CULTURAL AND LINGUISTIC ISSUES FOR ENGLISH LANGUAGE LEARNERS

Fall 2006

Number 1 in a Series of Monographs
Addressing Critical Issues in the Education of
English Language Learners

Funded in part by the Federation of
North Texas Area Universities

A project of the Bilingual/ESL Committee of the
Federation of North Texas Area Universities

Phap Dam, Ph.D.
Texas Woman's University
Series Editor

Melinda T. Cowart, Ed.D.
Texas Woman's University
Managing Editor

CULTURAL AND LINGUISTIC ISSUES FOR
ENGLISH LANGUAGE LEARNERS
Fall 2006

Phap Dam, Ph.D., Texas Woman's University
Series Editor

Melinda T. Cowart, Ed.D., Texas Woman's University
Managing Editor

Cover design by CANH NAM
Photo credits: *American Teacher* (an AFT publication)
Dao Thi Hoi, Ed.D.

Book design and Desktop publishing by VICANA

Printed and published by
CANH NAM Publishers, Inc.

Introduction

In the state of Texas the shortage of effectively prepared and certified bilingual and ESL teachers affects the education of language minority students on a daily basis. Thousands of linguistically diverse students endure entire school years without the services of highly qualified bilingual and ESL teachers. According to the 2004 American Community Survey of the U.S. Census, 32% of people five years of age and older in Texas speak a language other than English at home. In New Mexico that number increases to 36%, while in California the number of people speaking a language other than English at home rises to 41%. Yet, it has been estimated that fewer than 35% of teachers who work with the linguistically diverse student population have had any training in bilingual or ESL education.

The real world of school is one of cultural, linguistic, and academic diversity while the teaching force in the United States continues to reflect little diversity. Immigrant and refugee newcomers continue arriving in the U.S. for many reasons, including education, safety, opportunity and freedom. The children of immigrant and refugee parents live through an uprooting from all that is familiar and must face schooling that is frequently different from anything they may have previously experienced. Some children have never attended school before because of political, social or civil upheaval in their home countries or because their days have been spent literally running for their lives. In addition, the first, second, and third generations of American-born children of immigrants and refugees need to be taught by teachers who are not only knowledgeable of appropriate strategies but who also possess the cultural sensitivities to understand their unique experiences and necessities.

In order to compensate for the mismatch of a diverse student population and a teacher corps that lacks diversity, it is imperative that appropriate and effective teacher preparation and information be provided. Therefore, the Bilingual/ESL Committee of the Federation of North Texas Area Universities has prepared this monograph as a compendium of information about some of the most critical issues facing English language learners (ELLs) in the United States. Dr. Cowart provides insights into the uniqueness of the refugee experience and highlights what teachers should know about working with students who are refugees. Dr. Green provides a necessary overview of the English language learner in school by providing demographics and a discussion of current trends in the field of bilingual and ESL education. The articles by Dr. Robles-Goodwin, Drs. Midobuche and Benavides, and Dr. Wright address issues of appropriate programs and practice for enhancing the school achievement of ELLs. Dr. Mathis provides practical advice regarding the effective use of multicultural children's literature for all children, including the very diverse ELL population, and incorporates lists of appropriate books to use in the classroom. Effective strategies for supporting language growth in the first and second language are discussed in the articles by Dr. Sanchez and Dr. Garza. Dr. Dam provides a cogent analysis of some persistent errors in English made by Vietnamese speakers and suggests an instructional intervention for such interference errors. Dr. Rosado describes the sometimes close relationship of English and Spanish, providing multiple examples and characterizing the mutual impact each language has on the other as symbiotic in nature. A veteran bilingual educator, Dr.Deyoe-Chiullan, gives a lively update and discussion of current bilingual/ESL curriculum. Finally, Drs. Pemberton, Rademacher, and Anderson inform the reader about a growing phenomenon that touches virtually every group in the United States – that of grandparents raising grandchildren. Of particular interest are the recommendations for teachers that grandparents themselves offer.

The anticipated audience for the monograph is preservice and inservice teachers and administrators in addition to university faculty and students of ethnic, linguistic and academic diversity.

By creating a monograph regarding the effective teaching of culturally and linguistically diverse students, the Bilingual/ESL Committee seeks to inform preservice and inservice teachers as well as teacher educators about effective and best practices, current research and trends, and successful methods and materials.

While many journals and texts deal with theory, few are written in a manner that facilitates immediate comprehension and positive action. The information and strategies that are discussed in this publication are authoritative, concrete and applied in nature, with clear explanations of theory into practice. Because the monograph is intended for practical use by practitioners, every effort has been made to ensure that the language of the articles is scholarly, yet not intimidating. The strategies and ideas that are addressed should be readily useful to preservice and inservice teachers and university faculty.

Dr. Dam and Dr. Cowart, editors of the monograph, wish to thank the Federation of North Texas Area Universities and the Texas Woman's University College of Professional Education for their extensive support of this project. Their significant generosity enables the Bilingual/ESL Committee of the Federation to provide the monograph at no cost to educators and students.

It is essential to note that the current monograph is first in a series of monographs that will address the challenges and issues inherent in learning and teaching English as a second language. The Call for Manuscripts for the second monograph in this series appears at the end of this monograph. The editors remain dedicated to the continuation of this challenging and rewarding endeavor.

TABLE OF CONTENTS

From Killing Fields to Classrooms: Understanding and Teaching the Refugee Student

Melinda T. Cowart
Texas Woman's University

> It is too easy to imagine waking up on the moon where nothing looks the same or in a land where no one speaks your language.
>
> Imagine this instead.
>
> Imagine you have never heard of the Beatles. Or Mozart. Or Oprah Winfrey... You've never heard of Elvis... Imagine you don't celebrate birthdays..., Christmas, Chanukah, or New Year's on December 31.... You do not Trick or Treat....
>
> Imagine after having your homeland destroyed before your eyes, building a new life in a land where you have to learn a new language – one that is so self-referential – that you must learn not only the words, but the memories. Imagine coming to America.
>
> (Fiffer, 1991, pp. xv-xvi)

After working with refugee youth for more than two decades, both as an English as a second language teacher in a middle school classroom and as a youth group counselor for the Blue Dragon Explorer Post, a service organization comprised of Southeast Asian refugees and Asian immigrants and sponsored through Boy Scouts of America, I have come to realize that the teachers of newcomers have tremendous power to either nurture a successful school experience or to unknowingly allow a child to fail and fall through the cracks of the schooling system in the United States. Frequently, I observe that the end result, whether a child has a positive acculturation experience of learning to balance two cultures and languages, or endures a persistent feeling of being an outsider in American society, is directly related to the knowledge a teacher possesses about her students and the experiences and knowledge they bring into the classroom. Because newcomers are not members of any of the dominant groups in American society, they have a difficult time seeing themselves and their experiences in the school curriculum (Nieto, 2004). What newcomers do see of themselves in the classroom may be an inaccurate picture based on incorrect or missing information.

As the number of ethnically and linguistically diverse students in U. S. public schools continues to grow, the need for teachers who are equipped with the knowledge and skills necessary for effectively teaching diverse populations increases. While immigration patterns and refugee resettlement have changed significantly since September 11, 2001, the number of language minority students attending schools in the United States continues to increase in dramatic fashion, having increased by more than 100% between 1990 and 1999 (National Clearinghouse for Bilingual Education, 1999). Yet the number of teachers with any specialized training in Bilingual or English as a second language methodology has not grown to meet the demand (Waggoner & O'Malley, 1985; Hodgkinson, 2002). The increase in the culturally, linguistically, and academically diverse student population challenges teachers to acquire appropriate and precise information about the diverse experiences of their students so that they may teach in a manner that is culturally relevant and in a way that allows all students to see themselves reflected accurately and suitably in the curriculum. Without adequate preparation regarding the distinctive and varied experiences of newcomers as well as appropriate educational practice for their instruction, will the educators charged with providing equal educational opportunity for these students possess the awareness, the attitudes or the skills necessary for accomplishing the task? Will the teacher who lacks information regarding why and how refugees come to the United States be able to acknowledge and address each student's unique needs and requirements so that educational equity and success may be facilitated? The saying "one size fits all" simply does not apply in today's changing society and schools. In general, refugee students want their teachers to be well informed about what they have endured. In fact, they have noted that they feel a sense of isolation because their teachers and peers are unaware of even a small number of the changes they have had to undergo as refugees in a new land (Cowart, Wilhelm, & Cowart, 1998).

Acknowledging that perception governs how a teacher may respond and react to the complex needs of students who have been resettled as refugees in the United States, it is critical that all teachers have accurate knowledge of the facts of immigration and refugee resettlement. Thus, the purpose of this paper is two-fold – to enhance educators' knowledge regarding the refugee experience and to explore how to effectively and equitably address the exceptional needs of the children of refugees in U.S. public schools. Information and insights that have been acquired through much interaction with previous students, educators, and youth group members combined with what has been learned through intense study will be presented in an attempt to provide an accurate portrayal of the many aspects of the refugee experience. The following questions, among the most frequently asked by both preservice and inservice teachers, will be explored:

- What is a refugee?

- Why are refugees here and in U.S. classrooms?

- What is the process of refugee resettlement?

- What do refugees experience in the homeland, during escape, in the refugee camp, and in the new host country?

- How does the refugee experience impact learning and teaching?

Overview of refugee resettlement

Internationally, there were more than 11,500,000 refugees and asylum seekers during 2004. Thousands of refugees waited in refugee camps around the world, hoping that they would be able to join the resettlement process and be placed in a small number of countries that accept refugees for resettlement. The United States, Canada, Australia and Sweden led all other countries in the number of refugees that were admitted for resettlement, with the United States accepting more than any other country. Each year tens of thousands of newcomers enter the United States legally as refugees. In 2004 52,868 refugees from such countries as Ethiopia, Sudan, Afghanistan, Iraq, Somalia, Myanmar, and Vietnam were resettled in the United States (World Refugee Survey, 2005).

Thousands of children of refugees in America enter U.S. schools, eager to obtain a good education while learning English, the language of their new homeland. The regular arrival of new groups of immigrants, refugees and political asylum seekers adds to the diversity of English language learners (ELLs) in American schools. The newcomers bring with them unique experiences, languages and cultures that may become barriers in classrooms where teachers lack knowledge of diverse newcomer experiences and misinterpret the new students' choices, behaviors and attitudes. The children of refugees and asylum seekers in particular may have experienced multiple traumas in the homeland, during escape, in the refugee camp, and even in the new host country. They may have suffered torture, the loss of loved ones, exhaustion, and hunger. The experiences of newcomers and their reasons for coming to the United States vary, but their need for an effectual and just education is the unifying thread that binds immigrant, refugee and asylee together to present a formidable challenge to U.S. schools and educators.

What is a refugee?

Many people are familiar with the term "immigrant," but are unaware of how the definitions and experiences of immigrants and refugees differ. Law and Eckes (2000) have said that while an immigrant decides to reside in another country because the grass is greener, refugees flee to another country because "the grass is burning under their feet" (p. 64). The United Nations High Commissioner for Refugees (UNHCR) defines a refugee as a person outside of the United States who seeks protection on the grounds that to remain in the homeland would mean persecution or death because of race, religion, membership in a social group, political opinion or national origin. Thus, a refugee is someone who has fled across an international border in order to seek safe haven (World Refugee Survey, 2005). When large groups of citizens of a particular country plagued by political upheaval, ethnic cleansing, or life-threatening civil unrest must escape, the United Nations High Commissioner for Refugees is mandated to provide protection for refugees and to assist them in countries of asylum (UNHCR). Through their escape, refugees have severed all ties with their home countries and arrive in the refugee camps stateless and without the protection of any country. In contrast, an immigrant is an individual born in a foreign country who has sought and received permission to reside permanently in the United States (World Refugee Survey, 2005).

It is important to note that an asylee is similar to a refugee in that there is a well-founded fear of persecution if sent back to the home country. However, the asylee petitions the United States government for protection and legal recognition after entering the country while the refugee requests protection from outside of the United States. The asylum seeker must prove well-substantiated fear of persecution for the same reasons as the refugee. If granted asylum, the asylee is entitled to the same rights as a refugee, including legal residence in the U.S. and the potential to become an American citizen. Typically, the political asylee and the refugee have had similar experiences in the homeland, but have sought protection through different processes. It is essential to mention that political relationships between the United States and the countries of origin of the refugees and asylees may determine the process that must be followed in order to gain protection (Portes & Rumbaut, 1996).

Is it vital for educators to know whether a student is an immigrant, a refugee or a political asylee? Certainly, citizenship status is not a criterion for eligibility to receive exemplary instruction. However, there are particular experiences and even traumas that are inherent to each different immigration process. An educator who is knowledgeable about the obstacles and hurdles that a newcomer may have endured will more likely include some aspects of the newcomer's experiences, culture and language in the curriculum, being careful to not lump all immigrants into one group. Students are aware that they have not all had the same experiences and want their uniqueness to be recognized (Cowart, Wilhelm & Cowart, 1998).

> We are not all the same. We have different experiences. We
> have come for different reasons.
>> -- Aliya, Indian American student

What is the process of refugee resettlement?

When a crisis erupts in a particular country or region, the UN High Commissioner works with nearby countries to become countries of first asylum. Usually a refugee camp is set up to house, protect and begin processing those who have fled as refugees. The UNHCR may be represented by little more than a tattered United Nations flag atop a tent within sight of the war zone, yet it identifies a safe place to which displaced persons may flee. Within the refugee camp several actions must occur. First the refugee must register with the UN High Commissioner and the U.S. Embassy if he wishes to be resettled in the United States. Next the refugee is interviewed for the purpose of receiving official refugee status. A representative of the United States Customs and Immigration Service (USCIS) must also interview the refugee and bestow refugee status if the process is to continue. Once approved, the biographical data is sent to the national office of a refugee resettlement agency such as U.S. Catholic Charities, Lutheran Immigration and Refugee Services, or International

Rescue Committee. The resettlement agency enters into an agreement whereby the agency guarantees the U.S. Department of State that several basic services will be provided for the refugee and family members during the beginning resettlement phase. Prior to travel from the refugee camp, a refugee receives a medical clearance, a security clearance and a brief cultural orientation about the United States (U.S. Committee for Refugees and Immigrants). Of particular interest to educators and social service case workers is the fact that the cultural orientation tends to be quite inadequate in preparing refugees for the intricacies of their new membership in American society.

Subsequently, affiliates in approximately 25 primary resettlement sites around the United States receive the refugee and assume the responsibility for resettlement. During the first thirty days after arrival in the U.S., the resettlement agency works to find appropriate housing that is clean and safe and assists the refugee in registering with the Social Security Administration. In addition representatives from the agency enroll accompanying children in school, arrange medical evaluations, and help refugee adults find and enroll in ESL classes. In the award-winning film *Starting Over In America* produced by Public Broadcasting Services (PBS) in 1986, a group of young middle school students share their observations that it seemed as though the U.S. government was giving the refugee students and their families new cars, new homes, new clothes, and bigger, better stores. In reality, refugees receive only a few months of support through the resettlement agency. Afterwards there is no further financial assistance. In some instances congregations at some churches and synagogues sponsor families and provide additional support.

What do refugees experience in the homeland, during escape, in the refugee camp, and in the new host country?

Political unrest, ethnic cleansing, civil war, torture, hunger, starvation, loss of family members, and separation are only a few of the circumstances that lead individuals and families to escape their homelands. Refugee students have endured trauma of an intensity that only other refugees or combat veterans of war may share. Sometimes feelings and memories that have been suppressed may be expressed through something as innocent as a journal entry.

> My mom got her first child when she was twenty-five years old. It was a girl. She was the oldest child. Three years later my mom had a boy. He was the second child. A year later my mom was pregnant. The child was a girl. Then, a year later, my mom had her fourth child. It was a boy. Then the war started. When my oldest sister was twelve years old, she died because of hunger. Later on, the third and fourth child died, also of hunger. When my mom was six months pregnant, my dad died. The Khmer Rouge shot him. Three months later, I was born. We came to Dallas, Texas on April 4, 1984. Only my mom, her second child and her youngest, which is me, still lived and made it to the U.S.
>
> --Kamsath, a middle school ELL from Cambodia

Suddenly, escape becomes the only option. Leaving behind all that was once familiar and comfortable – ways of behaving, cultural practices and beliefs, and traditional values – refugees make the decision to flee to a place of safety in a country of first asylum.

The escape experience for many refugees is fraught with terror and danger, including enemy soldiers, land mines, and treachery from authorities seeking bribes. An encounter with a soldier during escape can lead to an instantaneous execution, assault or rape (Warwick, Neville, & Smith, 2006). Frequently, first attempts at escape are unsuccessful and sometimes have deadly consequences.

> It took us two days and two nights to get to the Thai border. We saw women raped by the Thai robbers along the way. In front of their families, in front of everyone. The robbers would come up and demand money or gold, and if you said that you didn't have anything, they would kill you. So we gave them everything along the way. We had so little. It was hard for us to believe – the Khmer Rouge were so bad and now the Thai robbers were so bad.
>
> --Paul Thai in Fiffer, 1991, p. 65

Typically a refugee has little time to prepare for escape. Most possessions, including important documents such as diplomas and family records are often left behind.

Once the decision is made to flee, virtually every refugee begins a process of uprooting. It is significant for children that they seldom have any control over the decision to leave. The decision to leave usually rests in the hands of adults. However, there are a few exceptions in which juvenile undocumented immigrants elect to flee abusive homes or homelands for a safer life in the United States. In an article in the *Dallas Morning News,* Rodriguez (2002) describes a case in which two young sisters fled their home in Mexico because of an impoverished and abusive mother who punished them by putting chili in their eyes. The little girls believed there was no alternative but to pack their favorite dolls, say a quick prayer, and float across the Rio Grande to safety in the U.S. In 2002 there were nearly 5,000 juvenile undocumented immigrants in the U.S., arriving primarily from Mexico, El Salvador, China, Honduras, and Guatemala (Rodriguez, 2002). Once here many of the young undocumented minors are placed in Bureau of Citizenship and Immigration Services detention centers until they can prove their need to be given asylum and be placed with family members or foster parents or be deported.

For all other children who are newcomers, including refugees, immigrants, and political asylees, the power to leave or stay in the homeland lies with parents or guardians. The lack of power and choice is part of the uprooting experience that Igoa (1996) characterizes as having six stages. The first three stages consist of mixed emotions, fear or excitement in the escape, and curiosity and generally occur prior to arrival in the new host country. A time of inner turmoil takes place upon learning that there will be a departure from home. The child is sad to leave behind friends and family, but is happy to go to a new and safe location. The escape occurs during the second stage and may be full of terror, crossing dangerous terrain with land mines and in the presence of enemy soldiers. Life in a refugee camp varies from camp to camp. Although the United Nations High Commissioner for Refugees is mandated to provide for the safety and basic needs of the refugees, the urgent nature of the refugee's escape makes it impossible to keep dangerous elements out of each camp. A school may exist, but teachers and materials are in short supply, leaving classrooms in refugee camps in short supply. Depending on world events and willing host countries, refugees may remain in refugee camps for months or decades. During the third stage of uprooting the child undergoes a time of curiosity regarding the new place and what the new life may hold. Fiffer (1991) tells a story about a refugee youth in a refugee camp who finds out that he and his family will be resettled in Dallas, Texas. The young man is very excited about the prospects until someone describes Dallas as a place not unlike the wild, Wild West where one might be shot by a cowboy in the middle of the street. Nevertheless, the patriarch of the family states that "he would rather be shot by a cowboy in America than by the Khmer Rouge in Cambodia" (p. 2). The young refugee indicates that his father's attitude helped the family have a positive attitude about going to America.

While the first stages of uprooting have a long lasting impact on the refugee child, it is the final three stages that provide the most opportunity for teachers to positively influence the newcomer in school and life. During the fourth stage the child may experience culture shock as the reality of attending school and learning in a new language becomes apparent. This stage is made more difficult by the mismatch of school and home language and culture. The newcomer doesn't understand school routines and feels isolated and lonely. Depression is common (Ooka-Pang, 2005).

> As for me, school was a nightmare. I felt nervous and was a little shy. After my mom and my brother left me there, I cried and cried until it was time for lunch. I didn't know what school was for me back then.
> --Kamsath, a middle school ELL from Cambodia

Stages five and six, assimilation or acculturation, into the mainstream are characterized by the uprooted child's choice, often greatly influenced by school experiences and peers, to either assimilate or acculturate. Warwick, Neville, and Smith (2006) state that the adjustment of refugee students may be helped or hindered by their daily experiences in the new host country. If the refugee student interprets the message of the school to be one of excluding diversity, the decision will be to assimilate and give up aspects of language and culture with the hope of finding acceptance among native-born American peers. Igoa (1996) states that if this occurs, the child may spend later years searching for an integrated sense of self. If the refugee student believes that participating in two or more cultures and languages is worthwhile and strives to maintain a balance through acculturation, the child will be more successful in the mainstream of American life.

These three stages of uprooting require an adjustment and an acclimation for the newcomer that can be greatly enhanced by a caring and well-informed teacher. It is critical that the child receive help and guidance to learn the new school program while at the same time experiencing a welcoming and accepting environment. If the message of the teacher and school is one of inclusion, assistance, and support, then the path to acculturation will be the logical choice for the child. However, if the refugee child perceives that his native language and culture are inferior in the eyes of the school, the decision may be to reject anything pertaining to home culture and language. Students, teachers and administrators in both formal and informal settings communicate the values and expectations of the school. Yet, students look to the teachers to set the tone for what is appropriate. Providing a welcoming, orderly, accepting and peaceful environment at school will assist young refugee students in dealing with their past experiences (UNHCR, 1994).

How does the refugee experience impact learning?

> Teachers need to realize that failing to stop stereotypical talk among other students is the same as condoning it.
>
> --Vijay, a high school student of Indian American heritage

> Everyday when I come home from school, my dad say do you have money for the electric? Do you have money send to your mom in Vietnam? That is why I cannot do my homework. I want to, but I have too much headache. So I just throw it.
>
> --Dong, former high school student from Cambodia

The refugee experience potentially has both an affective and academic impact on schooling. The academic impact may be due in part to an education that has been sporadic or non-existent because of war and political upheaval. Refugees have commonly endured a complete loss of services, including schooling, for a lengthy period of time prior to deciding to leave the homeland. Education while fleeing does not occur. Schooling in the refugee camps varies widely. Teachers are usually quite scarce, classrooms are overcrowded, and school supplies are difficult to obtain. It is rare that a refugee student arrives in a U.S. classroom without having missed weeks, months, or years of their schooling. In fact there are refugee students of middle school and high school age who enter public schools in the U.S. with no prior education (Hadaway, Vardell, & Young, 2002).

In addition there is a tremendous affective impact of the refugee experience. Depending on the number and severity of traumas suffered, the newcomer may be vulnerable to post traumatic stress disorder (PTSD) (Kemp &Rasbridge, 2004). They may experience depression, nightmares, flashbacks, sleeplessness, and loss of appetite. While the child senses that something is wrong, there is frequently the inability to describe the feelings and worries that are uncomfortable. In most instances the child does not possess sufficient proficiency in the English language to express deep feelings and fears. In addition, refugee children may perceive that no adult in the frantic world of school is interested in hearing their stories. In school PTSD serves to raise the student's affective filter, described by Krashen (Hadaway, Vardell, & Young, 2002) as attitudinal factors such as anxiety and fear that ultimately block learning. Typically, Krashen has referred to the classroom situation when considering the effects of a high affective filter. However, previous events, experiences and traumas greatly affect how a refugee child feels about a particular situation, including a classroom. If a child feels discomfort and anxiety from any source, the affective filter will be high and will serve to block learning.

Newcomer parents are often traumatized as well, having lost loved ones and homelands and may be unable to detect the symptoms of PTSD in their children. Thus, the parents may unknowingly exacerbate the situation by failing to provide the support, comfort and guidance that are so essential during this time (Cowart, Wilhelm, & Cowart, 1998). A lack of knowledge of available resources coupled with different cultural beliefs regarding mental health intensifies the problem (Kemp & Rasbridge, 2004).

Barriers to acculturation

Successful acculturation into a new society and culture involves a balancing of first language and native culture with the second language and new culture. Through this process of blending, both cultures and languages are respected and valid. The newcomer comes to realize that it is possible to participate in two or more cultures and speak two or more languages without having to give up substantial aspects of either one in order to fit in and belong (Law & Eckes, 2000). Newcomer students and their families usually encounter one or more barriers to acculturation, including language and cultural differences, mistrust of authorities, fear of retaliation, ignorance of laws, and a lack of advocacy (Cowart & Cowart, 1996).

Language difference is frequently cited by educators as a source of frustration for ELLs and their teachers (Ooka-Pang, 2005). When few educators have the knowledge and training necessary to plan and implement appropriate lessons and supporting activities that will facilitate language growth simultaneously with development of content knowledge, the anxiety of the ELLs along with the sense of inadequacy of unprepared teachers combine to create a barrier to acculturation. In the age of high-stakes testing and No Child Left Behind (NCLB) educators and administrators are tempted to look beyond the individual needs of newcomers who are learning English as a second language to the academic demands of tests and proof of adequate yearly progress (Cooper, Ramirez, & Cowart, 2005). While assessment and appropriate regular progress are essential, the language learning process, developmental in nature, is difficult to expedite. Portes and Rumbaut (1996) suggest that the educational plan for newcomers generally consists of rapidly leaving behind the first language while quickly learning the English language.   There are consequences to such a plan of action, the primary result being that the prior knowledge of the first language that would greatly assist in the learning of English and would augment the learning of others in the classroom is ignored (Cummins, 1994). Thus, students who possess a first language and may be literate in that language are encouraged to abandon the use of a vast resource for learning in school. When this occurs, once again, language difference is allowed to be a barrier to acculturation rather than a helpful tool for students and educators.

Another possible barrier to acculturation is cultural differences. Even the most educated refugees from large urban areas who have already experienced success in their homelands will encounter tremendous changes in cultural practice in the United States. For refugee families from very rural and isolated areas the different cultural practices, religious views, manner of dress, and standards for interpersonal relationships that they will find in the United States are frequently overwhelming. Law and Eckes (2000) have named several changes that ELL students experience, including the following:

- A change in geography or climate.

- A change from rural to urban settings.

- A change in the size of the living environment and/or the economic situation.

- A change in the culture of school.

- A change in social status or opportunities or goals.

- The change itself – traumatic and frequently life-threatening.

- A change in the language.

- A change in the way language is used.

- A change in their relationship with their parents (p. 63-65).

The school changes require much adaptation to the school setting while a great deal of adjustment to American society in general must occur. Refugee families often find that the role of parent and child is reversed because the child usually has more opportunity to learn English quickly. The children in these families must serve as interpreters at home, with the landlord, in doctors' offices and during parent conferences at school. Conflicts arise from the role reversal, particularly when a child is elevated to a position of authority he would not normally possess. In addition, the different cultural practices of refugees may make them targets for hostile comments, prejudice and even discrimination. The thoughtful educator will face a daunting task of assisting the refugee student with adjustment to American schools and life while at the same time protecting the student from uninformed and hurtful comments and actions. It is significant that the stresses caused by the mismatch of home and school culture will endure until acculturation, or the balancing of the first and second languages and cultures, takes place (Igoa, 1996).

Three other barriers to acculturation, mistrust of authorities, fear of retaliation, and ignorance of laws, pertain primarily to the parents of refugee students and do not apply specifically to the school setting, yet they impact the perception of refugees regarding what should occur at school. Refugees, accustomed to being harmed by those in positions of authority in the homeland, bring with them a fear that the same may occur in the United States.

While teachers represent authority, refugee parents from many cultures revere education and teachers, and truly trust educators to do what is right for their children. Outside of the realm of education, there exists a fear that if they complain about any problem or mistreatment, there may be a swift retaliation. Fiffer (1991) describes an event in which the patriarch of a refugee family, having been robbed of a black and white television during their first days in America, is coerced by another family member to report the incident to police. When a police officer arrives to take the report, the father tells the rest of his family to stay inside and lock the door so that even if he dies, the other family members would live. When the police were unable to find the stolen item, the family was still happy because the police officer was nice and did not harm them. The refugees' mistrust of authorities and fear of retaliation coupled with a general lack of knowledge of laws and appropriate practices in the United States work against a positive acculturation experience.

When new groups of refugees from various countries around the world are resettled in different sites in the United States, there may be no previously established group of people from the same countries and speaking the same languages to advocate for them. Thus, they may have a difficult time having a voice and expressing their needs and desires. Politically, the newcomers may remain virtually invisible for decades. While they are not actually invisible socially, a paucity of political clout tends to render them powerless within the schools and society. Forced to allow others to advocate for them, the lack of advocacy from members of their own group perpetuates a sense of helplessness over their own destiny. Anger and rebellion, against the new culture may result, thereby inhibiting the acculturation process (Nieto, 1994).

How may a teacher help refugee students to overcome these barriers to acculturation? First, it is essential to understand that many of the barriers are only barriers if they are allowed to be. An educator who comprehends the enormous task of learning English as a second language will use appropriate ESL strategies to make all instruction comprehensible. An approach to teaching that is highly interactive and utilizes a multitude of visual aids in a classroom that functions as an accepting haven will facilitate successful language growth. An appreciation of the complexities of the refugee experience will enable an educator to understand some of the behaviors and choices of refugee students and parents. Similarly, the knowledgeable teacher will invite the refugee experience as well as the cultural and linguistic experiences of newcomers into the classroom so that students may see themselves reflected in the curriculum and will believe that school is a place for them. Communication with the parents of refugee students, while challenging due to the language difference, must be a top priority. If parents are to understand what is expected of them and their children at school, they will need information in a format they can understand. Materials should be sent home in the first language of the parents. All meetings with parent groups should have interpreters for each language represented. It is the willingness to inform on the part of the educator that will enable the refugee parents to begin to trust authorities while no longer fearing retaliation. As newcomer families become aware of laws and common practices in the United States, they will start to have a voice and advocate for themselves and their children.

Recommendations for educators

- Remember that newcomers do not know what is expected of them in school. If they have attended school, their schooling may have been vastly different from that of U.S. public schools. Many students who are refugees will begin their formal schooling in America. Each teacher will need to teach school routines, practices and expectations.

- Refugee students in general arrive in the United States speaking another language. Whenever possible use the students' knowledge of their first languages as powerful resources in learning a new language and new content area information. Please note that students from Liberia do speak English and will simply need the help of teachers to adjust to the new host country.

- Find ways to facilitate the involvement of the parents of refugee students. The expectation of parental involvement is quite new for many newcomer parents. Translators for all communication may be necessary initially. The parents have much to offer and will gladly participate if they are able and if they are made to feel welcome.

- Avoid exacerbating cultural differences and conflicts. Among the greatest fears of the parents and grandparents of refugee students is that the young ones will forget their cultures and languages. Assist students in understanding that both the native culture and American culture are valid and have wonderful merits that should be celebrated.

- Incorporate materials, read alouds and activities that not only accomplish curricular objectives but also allow students to learn about themselves and others.

- Investigate the prior experiences of your newcomer students. Learn about their countries and the positive contributions their groups have made to the U. S. and the world. As one teen-aged Asian student stated, "We don't know about each other; we don't even know about other Asian cultures. And our teachers don't know about us either." (Cowart, Wilhelm, & Cowart, 1998, p.404).

- Create a safe, supporting environment that is respectful of all individuals in the classroom. Establish routines for most of what transpires in your classroom and teach those routines to the newcomers. This type of structure benefits all students and allows the newcomer to participate even when not everything is understood.

- Note that newcomers are unaware of the process of democracy and the unique aspects of American history. They simply have not been exposed to this information that Americans hold so dear. Therefore, teachers will need to plan lessons and activities that enable newcomer students to learn about democracy and the buildings, branches of government, agencies and historical details that make up American society.

- Remember that many cultures value the community over self. This will influence student behavior and preference, particularly for cooperative learning.

- Give non-English speaking newcomers the most important gifts of time and patience. The process of second language acquisition cannot be rushed. Newcomer students will need much time in order to learn enough English to be able to learn actively and independently, especially in a content area classroom.

Conclusion

Refugee resettlement will continue to impact the public school classrooms as long as the United States remains a beacon of liberty and freedom to oppressed people worldwide. The caring, knowledgeable, and insightful teacher of newcomers can facilitate an effective equitable education for newcomers while simultaneously enhancing the learning of other students in class. By so doing the teacher truly touches many futures – those of the students and those of members of American society. It has been suggested that no mystery exists regarding how to successfully teach all students. Many believe that educators already know all that is needed in order to help every child be successful. Refugee students in today's classrooms are among the custodians of the American society of tomorrow. A measure of assistance, support, and appropriate teaching from teachers today may impact not only the lives of refugee families in the United States, but also the quality of American life for decades to come.

References

Cooper, S., Ramirez, B., & Cowart, M. (2005). *The NCLB challenge and the ESL student: What now?* A paper presented at the TexTESOL 2005 State Conference, Dallas, TX.

Cowart, R. & Cowart, M. (1996). Communities held hostage: A profile of a Laotian street gang in Dallas. *Journal of Contemporary Criminal Justice, 12*(4), 307-315.

Cowart, M., Wilhelm, R., & Cowart, R. (1998). Voices from Little Asia: Blue Dragon teens reflect on their experiences as Asian Americans. *Social Education 62*(7), 401-404.

Cummins, J. (1994). The acquisition of English as a second language. In K. Spangenburg-Urbschat and R. Pritchard (Eds.), *Kids come in all languages: Reading instruction for ESL students* (pp. 36-62). Newark, DE: International Reading Association.

Fact Sheet No. 20, Human Rights and Refugees. Retrieved January 30, 2006 from the United Nations Office of the High Commissioner for Human Rights at www.unhcr.ch.

Fiffer, S. (1991). *Imagining America: Paul Thai's journey from the killing fields of Cambodia to freedom in the U.S.A.* NY: Paragon House.

Hadaway, N., Vardell, S., and Young, T. (2002). *Literature-based instruction with English language learners.* Boston: Allyn and Bacon.

Hodgkinson, H. (2002). Demographics and teacher education: An overview. *Journal of Teacher Education, 53*, 103-105.

How refugees come to America. Retrieved February 6, 2006 from U.S. Committee for Refugees and Immigrants at www. refugees.org.

Igoa, C. (1995) *The inner world of the immigrant child.* Mahwah, NJ: Lawrence Erlbaum Associates.

Kemp, C., & Rasbridge, L. (2004). *Refugee and immigrant health: A handbook for professionals.* Cambridge, UK: Cambridge University Press.

Law, B., & Eckes, M. (2000). *The more-than-just-surviving handbook: ESL for every classroom teacher.* Winnipeg, Canada: Portage and Main Press.

National Clearinghouse for Bilingual Education (1999). *The growing numbers of limited English proficient.* Washington, DC: U.S. Department of Education.

Nieto, S. (1994). *Affirming diversity: The sociopolitical context of multicultural education.* NY: Addison Wesley Longman.

Nieto, S. (2004). *Affirming diversity: The sociopolitical context of multicultural education.* NY: Pearson Education.

Ooka-Pang, V. (2005). *Multicultural education: A caring-centered, reflective approach.* NY: McGraw-Hill.

Portes, A, & Rumbaut, R. (1996). *Immigrant America: A portrait.* London, England: University of California Press.

Rodriguez, B. (2002, October 20). Uncertain journey. *The Dallas Morning News,* pp. A43.

United Nations High Commissioner for Refugees (1994). *Refugee children: Guidelines on protection and care.* Geneva, Switzerland: UNHCR.

Waggoner, D., & O'Malley, J.M. (1985). Teachers of limited English-proficient children in the United States. *The Journal of the National Association for Bilingual Education, 9*(3), 25-42.

Warwick, I , Neville, R., and Smith, K. (2006). My life in Huddersfield: Supporting young asylum seekers and refugees to record their experiences of living in Huddersfield. *Social Work Education, 25,* (2), 129-137.

World Refugee Survey (2005). Washington, DC: United States Committee for Refugees and Immigrants.

Major Demographics and Schooling Trends for English Language Learners and Their Teachers

Laura Chris Green
Texas A & M University -- Commerce

Introduction

English Language Learners (ELLs) are one of the largest groups of students in the United States, and they are also the fastest growing subpopulation. Sadly, although their needs are great due to their linguistic and cultural diversity, and their potential contributions to American society are just as great, due precisely to that linguistic and cultural diversity, they are the least well-served by our PK-12 public schools of any group, including special education students. Part of this lack of high quality services is due to a lack of resources, primarily a severe shortage of bilingual teachers and administrators, but it is also partly due to a lack of commitment to solving the problems currently encountered in our educational systems. Policy-makers such as legislators and school board members, educators in our public schools and in our teacher preparation colleges, parents and other citizens in the general population stubbornly adhere to myths about immigrants, ELL students, and bilingual and ESL programs that often lead to benign neglect at best and at worst to vehement attacks.

The data for this report is from a wide variety of sources including the 2000 Census, the US Department of Education, the National Center for Education Statistics, and professional books and journals. An effort was made to find both the most recent and credible sources of data, and often, for simplicity's sake, just one set of figures is presented if more than one was available. Figures were in most cases rounded as it is much easier to understand and interpret "over 5 million" than "5,203,485." And data were presented that relate specifically to English language learners rather than to minority students or to immigrants in general, although the latter kinds of data are indirectly related to ELLs and much more plentiful. For example, when examining issues of the under-representation of ELLs in gifted and talented (GT) programs, data on the representation of minority students, specifically African American and Hispanic students, were abundant, but figures for ELLs were sparse. So, although almost all ELLs are minority students, primarily Hispanics, the figures that prove the under-representation of minority students in GT programs were not reported, but rather only those figures that show the under-representation of ELLs in gifted and talented programs.

The report begins with the basics, how many ELLs there are, where they are, and how fast they are growing as a population—at furiously fast paces—and how they are moving into new areas of the country. The great diversity among ELLs with regard to languages spoken, countries of origin, race/ethnicity, and immigration status will be discussed. Data on which grade levels ELLs are in and numbers of ELLs receiving bilingual or ESL services are then presented followed by data on disproportionate representation in special programs. ELLs tend to be under-represented in GT programs while they are inclined to be over-represented in special education programs. The last section presents data on two important kinds of program resources, namely program funding and teacher qualifications, noting significant inadequacy in both areas. The paper concludes with a summary of all the data presented and a discussion of major implications for the field of bilingual education.

Over five million ELLs

The most recent data available from the US Department of Education indicates that there are over 5 million ELLs enrolled in American schools. Based on data collected in 2003-2004 from all 50 states, the District of Columbia, Puerto Rico, and the Pacific territories, the National Clearinghouse for English Language Acquisition (NCELA, 2005) reported that there were 5,013,539 ELLs enrolled in PK-12 public schools. For comparison purposes, this represented over 10% of the total enrollment of 48,616,090 students. Also for comparison purposes, for the 2002-2003 school year, approximately 6.5 million students, or 13.4% of all students, were classified as special education students (NCES, 2005).

Regional concentrations

Historically speaking, ELLs have primarily resided in the states where immigrants first enter the US, that is, states in the Southwest, Northeast, and Florida, home of many Cuban refugees since the 1950s. These areas still have high ELL populations, with six states and Puerto Rico reporting an enrollment of over 100,000.

Table I	
States and Territories with Over 100,000 ELLs	
State/Territory	ELLs
California	1,598,535
Texas	660,707
Puerto Rico	612,121
Florida	282,066
New York	191,992
Illinois	161,700
Arizona	144,145
Source: NCELA (2005)	

A few states are relatively small, but still have a large proportion of ELL students. There are five states, some large, some small, and Puerto Rico, which report high ELL student densities of at least 15%.

Table II	
States and Territories with Over 15% ELLs	
State/Territory	% ELL
Puerto Rico	99.9%
California	25.4%
New Mexico	16.9%
Alaska	16.3%
Texas	15.3%
Nevada	15.2%
Source: NCELA (2005)	

Great growth

Historically speaking, for decades the ELL student population has been growing much faster than the general student population.

This dramatic growth continues and in addition ELLs have moved into parts of the country, "the heartland," where they have rarely been seen up until now.

Overall growth in the ELL population nation-wide has been at least seven times as fast as that for all students. The same data source (NCELA, 2005) reported a 65% increase in ELLs in the US from 1993-94 to 2003-2004, i.e. in the last decade, and a 147% increase (more than double) from the 1989-90 figures, i.e. compared to 14 years ago. During the same time periods, the total school enrollment increased 7% from 1993-94 and 20% from 1989-90.

The states experiencing the most explosive growth in recent years are not the ones where ELLs have historically been in the past. Four of the five states that showed the higher percent increase during the last ten years are all located in the Southeast and the fifth, Indiana, is in the Midwest.

Table III	
States with the Highest Growth Rates in ELLs	
State	% Growth
South Carolina	522%
North Carolina	471%
Tennessee	448%
Indiana	438%
Georgia	398%
Source: NCELA (2005)	

As a result of this overall growth and the *diaspora* into new areas of the country, ELLs are now in all states and territories with 72% reporting enrollments of at least 10,000 ELLs. Only 8 states reported less than 5,000 ELLs and even these states, no matter how small, reported at least 1,000 ELLs.

Table IV	
States with Less Than 5,000 ELLs	
State	ELLs
Mississippi	4,681
Delaware	4,246
South Dakota	3,433
Wyoming	3,429
Maine	3,179
New Hampshire	2,755
West Virginia	1,594
Vermont	1,017
Source: NCELA, 2005	

A general consideration to keep in mind in looking at these figures is that probably the number of ELLs is undercounted in most states. The identification of ELLs begins with home language surveys, which ask parents what primary languages are spoken in the home. Many linguistically diverse parents will complete the surveys inaccurately, reporting that only English is spoken at home, because they believe that bilingual and ESL programs will harm their children or because someone (neighbors, principals, teachers) has influenced them to think so. In addition, most districts put intense pressure on teachers and students to move out of bilingual and ESL programs as quickly as possible, resulting in too early exits for many, perhaps most, students.

Diversity and homogeneity

American English Language Learners are a reflection of the incredible diversity present not only in the United States, but also in the world as a whole. They vary by country of origin, native language(s) spoken, race/ethnicity, and socio-economic status. The overwhelming majority, however, were born in the US and come from low-income, Spanish-speaking, Latino families.

Language diversity

The great diversity among ELLs is best seen by looking at the languages spoken by them. Based on a survey done by the Office of English Language Acquisition for the 2000-2001 school year, Kindler (2002) found that ELL students speak over 460 languages. Prominent among them are languages originating from East Asia, the Mid-East, Europe, islands in the Pacific, and Native-American tribes.

The great majority, 79%, speak Spanish, which, based on the 5 million total ELLs cited earlier, translates to approximately 4 million Spanish speakers. Asian languages are the next most common, with 2% of ELLs speaking Vietnamese, 1.6% speaking Hmong (an ethnic group from the mountain areas of Southeast Asia), 1% speaking Cantonese (a major dialect among the Chinese), and 1% speaking Korean.

See Table V for other languages with over 10,000 ELL speakers (rounded to the nearest thousand).

Table V		
Languages, Excluding Spanish, Spoken by over 10,000 ELLs		
Language Group	Language	No of Speakers
Asian	Tagalog (Philippines)	34,000
	Khmer (Cambodia)	27,000
	Mandarin (China)	22,000
	Lao	16,000
	Chinese (dialect/language not specified)	15,000
	Japanese	15,000
European	Haitian Creole (a French-based pidgin)	42,000
	Russian	37,000
	Portuguese	28,000
	Polish	12,000
	French	11,000
Mid-Eastern	Arabic	41,000
	Urdu (Pakistan)	19,000
	Serbo-Croatian	17,000
	Punjabi (India)	13,000
	Armenian	13,000
	Hindi (India)	11,000
Native-American	Navajo	27,000
	Native-American (unspecified)	10,000
Pacific Islander	Chuukese (Micronesia)	15,000
	Marshallese (Marshall Islands)	14,000
	Chamorro (Guam and Northern Marianas)	14,000
Source: Kindler (2002)		

Ethnicity and national origin

That 79% of ELLs speak Spanish means that the overwhelming majority of ELLs are Hispanic. There is great diversity among Latino ELLs, however, in terms of both country of origin and ethnicity. In 2000, of the 32.8 million Latinos living in the US, 66% were of Mexican origin, 15% were Central and South American, 9% were Puerto Rican, 4% Cuban, and 6% were "other Hispanic" (Díaz-Rico, 2004). The Urban Institute reports on the most common countries of origin for the children of immigrants by race/ethnicity (Capps, Murray, Ost, Passel, & Herwantoro, 2005). Among the top ten countries of origin for ELL students, six or 60%, including the top 3, are Spanish-speaking Latin American nations. The Urban Institute figures show that the origins of Hispanic children of immigrants as measured in the 2000 census were 60% from Mexico, 9% from Puerto Rico, 5% from El Salvador, 4% from the Dominican Republic, 2% from Guatemala, and 2% from Cuba.

The Urban Institute (Capps et al., 2005) gives us additional information on the races and countries of origin of the children of immigrants who are not Hispanic. The most common countries of origin for African American immigrants – Jamaica, Nigeria, Trinidad/Tobago, and Guyana – are English-speaking. The exception is Haiti, which, with 42, 000 Haitian Creole speakers, is the sixth largest language group among ELL students. Among children of Asian immigrants, the most common countries of origin are Vietnam, the Philippines, India, China, and Korea, in that order. The children of non-Hispanic European American immigrants are the second largest group after the children of

Hispanic immigrants, but most come from English-speaking countries (England and Canada) or have a high percentage of English speakers among their numbers. No data on the countries of origin for the fairly large number of Russian, Portuguese, Polish, and French speakers reported by NCELA among ELL students was found, although it can be assumed that Russia, Portugal, Poland, and France are the countries of origin for some. Brazil is a possible source of Portuguese-speaking immigrants while Canada and other former French colonies such as Algeria are likely origins for French-speaking newcomers.

Native-born and immigrant ELLs

A common myth is that most ELLs are foreign-born immigrants, the majority of whom are undocumented. In actuality, about three-fourths of ELLs were born in the US and only 10 to 15% appear to be illegal immigrants.

Kindler (2002) states that the states reported 1,127,172 immigrant students in PK-12 for the 2000-2001 school year. Even if all these immigrant students were ELLs, this represents less than 25% of the ELLs in PK-12. Capps, in looking at US data from the 2000 census, calculated that only 24% of immigrant students in grades PK-5 were first-generation immigrants born in other countries and only 44% of secondary students in grades 6-12. This fact is based on a variety of factors. First there are the many ELLs who are born into culturally and linguistically diverse families that are US citizens such as Native-Americans, Hawaiians, Puerto Ricans, Mexican Americans, and Pacific Islanders. Some of these families have been in the US for decades or even hundreds of years such as many American Indians, Puerto Ricans, and Mexican Americans. They live in long established communities, such as the Four Corners area belonging to the Navajo and the Rio Grande Valley area on the Texas/Mexico border, in which they are in the overwhelming majority such that their language and culture are the dominant ones in the area. Another key factor is that many immigrants are young and have their children after they arrive in the US. As a result, three fourths of the children of immigrants are US-born (Capps, 2001).

Among the estimated 1.1 million ELLs who are foreign-born immigrants, it is impossible to know how many have legal versus illegal immigration status. In addition to the general logistical difficulties of trying to identify and count illegal immigrants, the 1982 US Supreme Court decision, *Plyler vs. Doe*, prohibits schools from denying undocumented students a free public education and from requiring students or parents to document their immigration status. This includes requiring them to provide social security numbers or other forms of identification that can be used to establish immigration status. With the understanding that counting illegal immigrants is especially problematic, it is noted that Capps (2005) estimates that approximately half of the foreign-born immigrant students are undocumented aliens. This would mean that somewhere around 10 to 13% of ELLs are undocumented.

Parental socioeconomic status

Approximately twice as many ELL students come from low-income families as do English proficient students. Capps (2005) reports that 68% of elementary ELLs were in families that were on free or reduced lunch status as compared to 36% of English speakers, and at the secondary level 60% as compared to 32%. These percentages can also be compared to those of European American, non-Hispanic students who had poverty rates in 2000 of 26% at the elementary level and 22% at the secondary level.

The 2000 Census also revealed that the parents of limited English proficient children had lower levels of educational attainment than English proficient children as shown both by a lack of high school degrees as well as not even reaching the ninth grade of school. Table VI summarizes the figures that compare the parents of ELLs to those of English proficient students for the above three socioeconomic status indicators.

Table VI Socioeconomic Status of the Parents of ELLs Compared to the Parents of English Proficient Students				
	Elementary Level		Secondary Level	
	ELLs	English Speakers	ELLs	English Speakers
Low-income	68%	36%	60%	32%
No HS degree	48%	11%	35%	9%
Did not reach 9th grade	25%	2%	26%	4%
Source: Capps et al (2005)				

Also of note are the high poverty rates and low educational attainment levels of the parents of young Hispanic children in grades PK-5. Hispanic children show the lowest socio-economic status indicators, regardless of their citizenship or immigration status, followed by African American children, then European

American, then Asian American (American Indians were not included in this analysis as they are not immigrants).

Table VII		
Socioeconomic Status of the Parents of Hispanic Children in PK - 5		
Citizenship Status	Low Income	No HS Degree
Foreign-Born	76%	59%
Born in US to Immigrants	66%	40%
Born to US Citizens	51%	6%
Source: Capps et al (2005)		

More ELLs in elementary schools

The number of ELLs steadily declines as they move up the grades, a clear indicator that many are exited from bilingual and ESL programs every year. Whether all of these students are ready to transition into full English-only mainstream classrooms is a key question for bilingual education policy makers, but policy issues aside, the pattern is clear.

Sixty-seven percent of the 4.6 million ELLs reported by the Office of English Language Acquisition (NCELA, 2002) were in grades PK-6 and 31% in grades 7-12. Two percent were classified as "ungraded, other, and not specified." Another breakdown shows over 44% in the primary grades (PK-3), although this number is probably underestimated as some state education agencies did not report prekindergarten enrollments. Over a third (35%) were in the middle grades (4-8), and 19% were enrolled at the high school level. Figure 1 shows the progression across the grades of ELLs in terms of percentages.

Figure 1
Percentage of ELLs at Primary, Middle, and High School Levels

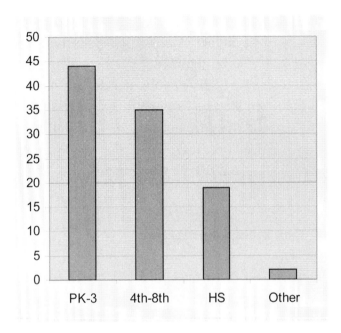

Source: NCELA (2002)

Unfortunately, the lower numbers at the high school level are also due to high drop out rates as well as exiting from the programs as students move up the grades. The National Center for Education Statistics (NCES, 2004) found that 27 percent of Hispanic 16- through 24-year-olds were not enrolled and had not completed high school in 2001. Even higher than the rate for all Hispanic students was the rate of 43% for Hispanics born outside the US. It is assumed that almost all of these Hispanic immigrants are ELLs. More recently, Johnson (2005) reported that the high school attrition rate for Texas was 48% for Hispanic students for the 2004-2005 school year. His analysis did not look at Hispanic immigrants specifically, but an assumption that the attrition rate for them would be even higher than for all Hispanic students is in order. There may also be significant numbers of older ELLs who never enter American high schools and so are not captured in dropout and attrition studies. For one thing, in most states, if they are over 16 years old, they are not required to enroll in school. For another, they may be "under the radar" due to illegal immigration status and/or being engaged in working full time and so not in school.

More ESL than bilingual programs

The data suggest that almost all ELLs have been in schools in which they received bilingual or ESL services of some kind. This can range, of course, from complete daily full-time programs to being pulled out of a regular classroom once a week for an hour by an ESL teacher. Reporting on data for 1993-94, the National Center for Education Statistics (NCES, 1997) states that only 3% of LEP students were not receiving any special language services of any kind. The same report stated that 85% of schools had ESL programs and 36% had bilingual programs. Since these two percentages add up to more than 100%, many schools either enrolled their ELLs in both kinds of programs, or, a more likely situation, based on parent choice or on the language spoken by the child, enrolled some ELLs in bilingual programs and others in ESL programs within the same school.

Another source of data from the 2000-2001 school year (Kindler, 2002) reported that 22.7% of ELLs received instruction that incorporated the child's native language and that 53.9% received instruction exclusively in English. Rather puzzling is that the language of instruction was not reported for the unusually large percentage of 23.4% of ELLs, including no data received on this topic from Florida, Puerto Rico, and the Pacific Islands. Like the data from the 1997 report, however, it is not clear how to interpret the term "instruction incorporates native language" in terms of quantity or quality. Does this mean that the school teaches children to read in the native language and provides content area instruction in L1, a relatively strong usage of native language instruction? Or does it mean that teachers occasionally use L1 for clarification, translating individual terms for students or providing them with bilingual dictionaries, a weaker usage of native language instruction?

Current disproportionate representation data

Although state and national legislation now require fair, nondiscriminatory identification of students for both kinds of special programs, disproportionate representation continue for both. Current statistical evidence shows mixed results for special education programs and clear results of under-representation for GT programs.

Hopstock and Stephenson (2003) did an analysis of the limited English proficient student data collected from school districts for the Office of Civil Rights. The nation-wide percentage of LEP students eligible for special education services was 7.9%.

Compared to the previously cited figure of 13.4% of all students eligible for special education services (NCES, 2005), this would seem to indicate a clear pattern of under-representation in special education, but examination of the data by states shows a wide range of figures, from a high of 17.3% in North Dakota to a low of 0.7% in West Virginia. Ten years earlier, Henderson, Abbot, and Strang (1993) reported similar national disparities among the states with a high of 26.5% in Massachusetts to lows of under 1% in Colorado, Maryland, and North Carolina. Taking the data down to the next level looking at districts, Robertson, Kushner, Starks and Drescher (1995) found that some Texas districts had five times the rate of ELLs in special education as other districts in Texas.

Additional data from Hopstock and Stephenson (2003) suggest that under-representation rather than over-representation may be the more common situation at the present time. Table VIII compares the percentage of all students and LEP students by disability categories:

Table VIII Percentage of Students in Special Education by Disability Category		
Disability Category	Percentage of All Students	Percentage of All LEP Students
Mild retardation	0.9%	0.3%
Moderate retardation	0.3%	0.2%
Severe retardation	0.1%	0.2%
Emotional disturbance	0.9%	0.2%
Learning disabled	6.1%	4.7%
Developmental delay	0.2%	0.1%
Source: Hopstock & Stephenson (2003)		

Firm conclusions as to either over-representation or under-representation of ELLs in special education at the national level cannot be made because of the great variety among reporting agencies. It would appear that many states, districts, and most probably schools are over-identifying these students for services and many others are under-identifying them. The causes for both scenarios can only be speculated on. Causes for under-identification appear to stem from school districts' fears that they will be cited for discriminating against minority students and ELLs by placing too many in special education programs. In attempting to avoid this, school districts may over-compensate, issuing formal and informal edicts that few or no diverse students can be referred for services. They may also make the process so difficult and cumbersome that teachers and other school staff routinely avoid it. Finally, a lack of staff resources, specifically a severe shortage of bilingual diagnosticians, makes complying with the law problematic at best.

The data for ELL participation in GT and other programs that target high ability students are much clearer than the data for special education programs. Hopstock and Stephenson (2003) found that 1.4% of LEP students were enrolled in GT programs as compared to 6.4% of all students. The under-representation was highest at the middle school level (1.6% versus 9.2%), next highest at the high school level (1.7% versus 7.8%), and lowest at the elementary level (1.3% versus 4.8%). These rates as a whole reveal that ELLs are approximately five times less likely to be in GT programs as are all students. The same study reported that for ELLs who were seniors in high school, 1.0% were enrolled in advanced placement (AP) math courses and 0.8% in AP science courses. For all high school seniors from the reporting schools, 3.2% were enrolled in AP math and science courses.

State, local, and federal funding

Although opponents of bilingual programs often argue that the programs are prohibitively expensive, the actual figures suggest that in most places the programs are seriously under-funded. Schools receive their operating funds from local, state, and federal sources. In 2001-02, the 50 states and the District of Columbia spent an average of $7,734 per student (Cohen & Johnson, 2004). Almost 43% were from local funds, 49% from state funds, and 8% from federal funds. Local funds are frequently based on property taxes. As the majority of ELLs are from low-income families and often live in low-income neighborhoods, many live in school districts which find it difficult, if not impossible, to adequately fund their schools without assistance. Bilingual and ESL programs have traditionally relied on outside funding from states and federal agencies to meet their extra costs and to lessen the funding gap.

Prior to the passage of the *No Child Left Behind Act* in 2002, federal funding for innovative bilingual education programs was awarded through a competitive grant process under Title VII of the *Elementary and Secondary Education Act.* Since then, each state has received funds based on LEP student counts which they then distribute to school districts. Over 110 billion dollars were distributed by the US Department of Education in 2005 for all the educational programs that it funds. A slight increase is proposed for 2006 to 116 billion dollars. By contrast, 676 million dollars were awarded in 2005 to school districts with ELL students and the same amount is proposed for 2006. This translates to approximately $133 per student (NABE, 2005). Another comparison can be seen by observing that there has been a 36% increase in the total federal educational budget since 2002 and a 2% increase in the funding for ELLs.

We can also look at special state funding provided to districts with ELL students to fund their programs. The Education Commission of the States randomly surveyed ten states to determine how they funded their ELL programs (ECS, 2002). The results for selected states who responded are in Table IX.

Table IX Funding for ELLs Provided As Reported by Selected States		
State	Funding per Student	Total Funding Rounded to nearest million
California	$ 100	$ 53 million
Florida	$ 905	*$ 23 million
Maryland	$1,350	$ 30 million
New York	$1,102	$ 53 million
Texas	$ 776	$ 71 million
New Jersey	$ 240	*$120 million
Source: ECS (2002) *These figures were estimated		

Teacher shortages

Multiple sources reveal a profound shortage of bilingual and ESL teachers in the nation. In greatest demand are bilingual teachers at the elementary level and teachers for students in urban areas. In 1994, the General Accounting Office reported a shortage of 175,000 bilingual teachers at the national level (GAO, 1994). In their survey of large city school districts and colleges of education, the Urban Teacher Collaborative (2000) found that 72.5% reported an immediate shortage of bilingual teachers and 67.5% cited an immediate shortage of ESL teachers. More recent data collected from Texas school districts for the 2001-2002 school year found that the districts were unable to fill 26% of open secondary bilingual/ESL positions throughout the school year and reported a shortage of 2,906 teachers in the elementary bilingual/ESL area (Lara-Alecio, Galloway, Palmer, Arizpe, Irby, et al., 2003). The American Association for Employment in Education in their wide-scale survey of US teacher preparation institutions (AAEE, 2002) calculated an average demand of 3.96 for ESL teachers (on a 5 point scale) and of 4.10 for bilingual teachers, exceeded only by the demands calculated for math teachers (4.28), physics teachers (4.26), chemistry teachers (4.20), and special education teachers (ranging from 4.59 to 4.19 depending on the specialization area).

Summary and implications

This document has presented facts and figures about English language learners, their schools and educational programs, and the teachers who serve them. Perhaps in the environment of the current education reform efforts which are largely data-driven, both advocates for and opponents of bilingual education can calmly examine the numbers and come to reasoned, fair decisions about how best to address the issues before us, issues which no amount of denial or wishful thinking will make go away.

Table X provides a concise summary of the facts and figures presented in the complete report. Following the table the facts are summarized and relevant implications of the data and recommendations for educators and policy makers are stated.

Table X Key Facts and Figures for ELL Students
Total numbers nation-wide (includes 50 states, DC, and territories): Over 5 million ELLs
Growth: 7 times faster than all students, averaging around 10% annually Greatest growth areas: Southeastern and Midwestern states
Total number of languages: Over 460 spoken Most common language: ~ 4 million Spanish speakers, 79% of the total Other major language groups: East Asian, Mid-Eastern, European, Pacific Islander, American Indian
Top ten countries of origin (in order): 1. Mexico, 2. Puerto Rico, 3. El Salvador, 4. Vietnam, 5. Dominican Republic, 6. Guatemala, 7. Haiti, 8. Korea, 9. Philippines, 10. Cuba
Country of origin: 76% born in the US, 24% foreign-born In US legally: 87 to 90% citizens or legal immigrants, 10 to 13% undocumented immigrants

Family income levels: Poverty rate of 68%, 2 times as high as for English-speaking peers
Parents with no high school degree: 45%, almost 5 times as high as for English-speaking peers
Parents < 9th grade: 25%, over 10 times as high as for English-speaking peers

Elementary vs. secondary: 67% in PK-6, 31% in grades 7-12

ELL services: 85 to 97% of ELLs receiving some kind of ELL services
In bilingual or ESL programs: 85% of schools ESL programs, 36% bilingual programs

In special education: 7.9% vs. 13.4% for all students, individual states from 0.7% to 17.3%
In GT programs: 1.4 % vs. 6.4% for all students, almost 5 times lower

Per capita funding from state sources: High of $1350 in Maryland to low of $100 in California, compare to $7,734 expenditure per student for all students
Federal funding: $676 million, $133 per student, a 2% increase since NCLB passed in 2002

Teacher shortages: 175,000 bilingual teachers needed

Implications and recommendations

- Representing over 10% of all students in PK-12, ELLs are a population which should not be ignored. Our country needs to give immediate serious, sustained, and substantial attention to addressing their needs. This would include educators in all parts of the country, teacher preparation institutions, legislators and policy makers, and state and federal education agencies.

- As four out of five ELLs speak Spanish, bilingual services should be provided to Spanish speakers whenever possible. Fortunately, as one of the top three languages spoken in the world and in the Western hemisphere, there are many print and web resources easily available to support this and many Spanish speakers already within our national borders.

- Bilingual services are the preferred mode for the speakers of other languages as well, but schools may not be able to provide them due to a lack of resources. In such cases, programs that provide day-long regular access to trained, certified ESL teachers and/or to sheltered content area teachers should be implemented.

- If tomorrow morning Americans managed somehow to completely close the borders to illegal immigrants through immigration reform as currently proposed by many policy makers and legislators, there would still be a large and fast growing population of ELLs in the US. In other words, the challenge is never going to just disappear.

- In addition, most ELLs are citizens or legal residents, which means they have as much right to a free and equitable public education as anyone else. Almost all will remain in the US their entire lives. They need to become productive contributors to our economy and to our democratic way of life. This can only be accomplished through providing them with a high-quality education that helps close the current achievement gap.
- The families of ELLs will often struggle with the daily demands of life in poverty. Parents may have to work two jobs and will not be able to provide their children with many material things like books, computers, and family vacations which can facilitate academic learning. Schools should give considerable attention to addressing needs that arise due to poverty.
- The families of ELLs will need assistance in learning to navigate the PK-12 educational pipeline in our American schools. Most parents want their children to be more successful in life than they were, so this means they want them to graduate from high school and preferably go to college, but low-income, uneducated parents usually do not know how to go about doing this (Robledo-Montecel, Gallagher, Montemayor, Villareal, Adame-Reyna, & Supik, 1993). Teachers and counselors should maintain high expectations for ELL students. Information on how to better prepare for a college education as well as how to secure funding through scholarships should be made available.

- Schools need to work in partnership with families. Regular, bilingual communication between school and parents and meetings in which translators are provided should be the norm. Family literacy, homework assistance, and after school programs are other ways schools can play crucial roles in improving school-home relationships.

- Critics who say that ELL students stay in bilingual and ESL programs "too long" are not aware of the facts. Students routinely leave the programs as they go up the grades, as the numbers clearly indicate. Immigrant children continue to enter our schools at all grade levels, so as students move out of the programs they are often replaced by recent immigrants. Schools should be recognized for their efforts on behalf of ELLs, and educators should concentrate on how to improve bilingual and ESL programs rather than trying to dismantle them.

- Although the numbers are smaller than for elementary school, a substantial number of ELL students enter American schools at the secondary level. In addition to facing a more challenging curriculum in a language they don't understand, secondary students have fewer years left in which to catch up to their English-speaking peers. This occurs at an age in which they are trying to establish their cultural and social identities. Secondary programs should be provided more resources for their ELLs, including training for regular content area teachers in the delivery of sheltered instruction, additional bilingual and ESL staff, and additional instructional materials. Schools should also consider providing bilingual programs instead of just ESL programs at the secondary level as they have been shown to more quickly and effectively facilitate both English language acquisition and content area learning (Ovando, Collier, & Combs, 2006).

- As public schools seem to be doing a fairly decent job providing services to most ELLs, they should now focus on insuring that those services are of sufficient quantity and quality to make a real difference. As long as ESL services are more prevalent than bilingual services, academic achievement will not be maximized for ELLs. Policy makers should support as much as possible the provision of an adequate quantity as well as quality of services.

- All districts should look at the representation of ELLs in their special education and GT programs. If they find significant over- or under-representation, they should examine their policies and procedures for special programs referrals, ensuring that they comply with the principles of valid dual language assessment and avoiding both linguistic and cultural bias. Above all, they should make sure that neither formal nor informal policies discourage nor prohibit referral of ELLs to either kind of program. They may also need to recruit bilingual diagnosticians for their staffs.

- All teachers need training on the identification and referral processes for ELL students for both special education and GT programs. This training should become a regular part of all teacher preparation programs and be provided by districts to inservice teachers. The focus of the training should be on valid dual language assessment and could strengthen their classroom instructional programs as they learn how to use authentic assessment methods to make decisions about what and how to teach.

- Additional resources should be allocated by states and the federal government to school districts, teacher preparation institutions, researchers, and those seeking bilingual or ESL pre-service or inservice training. This would include additional funding for bilingual and ESL teacher scholarships, inservice teacher training, research studies to identify best practices, and bilingual and teacher recruitment initiatives.

- All teachers should acquire basic knowledge of ESL methods and techniques and understand the principles and purposes of culturally responsive teaching. This training, like the training recommended on dual language assessment, should become a regular part of all teacher preparation programs and be provided by districts to inservice teachers.

Conclusion

English language learners currently constitute over 10% of the total school population, and they are in classrooms in every part of the nation. Their numbers grow year after year, but the achievement gap between them and their English-speaking peers never lessens. Teachers, university professors, parents, and policy makers need to work together to better meet their needs. Providing long-term, quality bilingual programs to more of the 79% of ELLs who are Spanish speakers would help significantly. Wherever possible, bilingual services should also be provided for non-Spanish-speaking ELLs. ESL instruction within both bilingual and ESL programs should also be improved. Finally, all teachers and administrators, including those who speak only English, should learn more about how to assess and modify instruction for ELLs.

References

AAEE (2002). *Educator supply and demand in the United States.* Columbus, OH: American Association for Employment in Education. Available from http://209.235.214.188/pdf/SDReport02.pdf

Baldwin, A. Y. (1985). Programs for the gifted and talented: Issues concerning minority populations. In F.D. Horowitz & M. O'Brian (Eds.), *The gifted and talented: Developmental perspectives*, (pp. 223-250). Washington, DC: American Psychological Company.

Capps, R., Fix, M., Murray, J., Ost, J. , Passel, J., & Herwantoro, S. (2005). *The new demography of America's schools: Immigration and the No Child Left Behind Act.* Washington, DC: The Urban Institute. Available from http://www.urban.org/publications/311230.html

Capps, R. (2001). Hardship among children of immigrants: Findings from the 1991 national survey of America's families. *Assessing the new federalism* (Policy Brief B-29). Washington, DC: The Urban Institute.

Cohen, C. & Johnson, F.(2004*). Revenues and expenditures for public elementary and secondary education: School year 2001-02.* Washington, DC: National Center for Education Statistics. Available from http://nces.ed.gov/pubs2004/rev_exp_02/#5

Díaz-Rico, L. (2004). *Teaching English language learners: Strategies and methods.* Boston, MA: Pearson Education.

ECS (2002). *A survey of state ESL funding systems.* Denver, CO: Education Commission of the States. Available from http://www.ecs.org/clearinghouse/31/95/3195.htm

GAO (1994). *Limited English proficiency - A growing and costly educational challenge facing many school districts.* Washington, DC: General Accounting Office.

Gould, S. J. (1981). *The mismeasure of man.* New York: W. Norton.

Henderson, A., Abbot, C., & Strang, W. (1993). *Summary of the bilingual education state education agency program survey of states' limited English proficient persons and available educational services.* Arlington, VA: Development Associates.

Hopstock, P.J. & Stephenson, T.G. (2003). *Descriptive study of services to LEP students and LEP students with disabilities.* Arlington,VA: Development Associates, Inc.

Johnson, R. (2005, October). Little improvement in Texas school holding power: Texas public attrition study, 2004-05. *IDRA Newsletter*, pp. 1-8, 12-13. Available from http://www.idra.org/Newslttr/2005/Oct/Roy.htm#Art1

Kindler, A. L. (2002). *Survey of the states' limited English proficient students and available educational programs and services, 2001-2002 summary report.* Washington, DC: National Clearinghouse for English Language Acquisition and Language Instruction Educational Programs. Available from http://www.ncela.gwu.edu/policy/states/reports/seareports/0001/sea0001.pdf

Lara-Alecio, R., Galloway, M., Palmer, D., Arizpe, V., Irby, B.J., Rodríguez, L., & Mahadevan, L. (2003). *Study of bilingual/ESL teacher recruitment and retention in Texas school districts.* College Station, TX: Texas A & M University. Available from http://ldn.tamu.edu/Archives/recruitmentretention.pdf

Understanding English Language Learners: Challenges and Promises

Patsy J. Robles-Goodwin
University of North Texas

Current and future teachers and school administrators are being faced with a challenge that is not likely to change in the near future. The number of students entering public school classrooms in the United States speaking a first language other than English is on the increase. Many large urban school districts are challenged with the many different languages spoken by their students and families (Hildebrand, Phenice, Gray, & Hines, 2000). Suburban and rural schools are also experiencing an increase of students speaking English as a second language (ESL). In the United States between 1986 and 1998, the number of children with limited English proficiency rose from 1.6 million to 9.9 million. It is estimated that by the year 2050, the percentage of children in the United States who arrive at school speaking a language other than English will reach 40% (Lindholm-Leary, 2000). The impacts of these demographic changes are challenging educators and administrators to provide academically appropriate and challenging instruction for all English Language Learners (ELLs). Many of these students may come from backgrounds of poverty which impact their educational quality and attendance and also may have parents with low levels of education (Espinoza-Herold, 2003). The schools they attend may be dealing with limited resources and have insufficient numbers of certified teachers, who would have the knowledge of how to best educate ELLs. The reality is that many teachers do not have specialized training on best instructional practices as it relates to cultural diversity or culturally responsive instruction. Gay (2000) defines culturally responsive teaching as using the cultural knowledge, prior experiences, and performance styles of diverse students to make learning more appropriate and effective for them. It emphasizes the strengths of students. Culturally Responsive Teaching is a pedagogy that recognizes the importance of including students' cultural references in all aspects of learning (Ladson-Billings, 1994). The purpose of this article is to briefly address the challenges of educating English language learners (ELLs), shed light on the confusion many educators have between bilingual and ESL programs in regard to the programs' roles and functions, provide research regarding learning a second language, and provide practical and effective instructional strategies that will be helpful for current and future teachers and administrators challenged to provide quality educational programs for ELLs.

Although studies in the past have recommended that students be instructed or supported in their first language and given five to seven years to become academically prepared, the reality is that ELLs are typically expected to learn English in a couple of years to a level of being able to take and successfully pass standardized and state-mandated tests (Collier, 1987; Cummins, 1981; Krashen, 1981). When ELLs are given some type of English assistance and then are not able to attain the academic expectations, the program, teacher and/or the student are labeled unsuccessful. The inability to instruct ELL students with successful outcomes is a frustration voiced by many educators today when challenged to work with them (Ovando & Collier, 1998). These educators express frustration and feel their prior university coursework has not prepared them sufficiently for working with culturally diverse populations and their families, as well as in the instructional realm (McCandless, Rossi, & Daugherty, 1996). Therefore, many hit-and-miss instructional strategies in experimental mode are used everyday by educators across America in classrooms with ELLs in the hope that one or two strategies will work.

Understanding the language acquisition process and development, and research-proven instructional strategies for working with ELLs is essential for successful teaching and learning. If teachers really want to be successful and effective, literacy instruction for ELLs should be very deliberate, organized, and strategic, so that they learn the language system while learning to read and write in English. The educator should view the student's knowledge of another language as a valuable asset and not as a liability to becoming literate in English (Baker, 1996; Samway & McKeon, 1999). The instructional modus operandi should not be mediocre or compensatory. For ELLs, it is important to build on first-language competencies rather than to assume that ELLs have few language strengths requiring a remedial approach for learning (Freeman & Freeman, 1993). For many ELLs at the elementary level, two language programs may be available, Bilingual Education (BE) and ESL. Some schools refer to their ESL program as English to Speakers of Other Languages (ESOL). Many educators confuse the function and purpose of these two programs. How are they alike? How are they different? Both programs are used to educate ELLs.

Bilingual education programs

Bilingual programs use *two* languages for instructional purposes, the student's first language and English. The first language used in bilingual programs is usually dependent on the geographical location of students and their families. For example in the south, especially in Texas, most bilingual education programs use Spanish and English. While there are different types of bilingual education models, many school districts tend to implement a transitional model that offers first language (L1) support but whose ultimate goal is for students to learn English as a second language (L2). In other words, maintaining the student's first language is not the goal of a transitional bilingual program (Ovando & Collier, 1998). Students are given initial language support in order to learn English. Most bilingual programs can be found at the lower grade levels from prekindergarten up to third or fourth grade. If ELLs have been in a bilingual program since prekindergarten, they are usually expected to exit or transition into a "regular" English-speaking classroom by third or fourth grade (Crawford, 1991). The bilingual education teachers are expected to be literate and proficient in the first and second language (English) of the students. Therefore, bilingual teachers attain their teaching credentials similar to "regular" or generalist teachers, but they are required to demonstrate proficiency in the other language of the bilingual program and to take classes that will prepare them to work with ELLs. It is believed students in bilingual education

classes will not fall behind in their studies due to instruction in
their first language. In other words, instructional time is not lost
due to the students' inability to understand or speak English. Since
the transitional model of bilingual education emphasizes English
proficiency, ESL strategies are used by the bilingual teacher. The
teacher's instruction is only in English during the ESL portion of
class time. The teacher uses many different types of strategies such
as visuals and oral language to facilitate the learning of English
(Ovando & Collier, 1998).

Characteristics of effective biliteracy programs include a
strong academic curriculum in bilingual education; well defined
instructional plans and strategies to teach reading and writing;
strong administrative support; strong support for first-language
instruction as a bridge to learning English; strong language and
reading transfer strategies; and the belief that literacy is a vital skill
that enables individuals to function in society (August & Hakuta,
1997). Effective biliteracy programs also emphasize reading,
writing, oral, and listening comprehension with the conviction that
listening and speaking a language cannot be separated from the
process of learning decoding and written communication skills in
the first and second languages (Jiménez, García, & Pearson, 1996;
Tinajero & Devillar, 2000).

With all the promises of well-implemented bilingual programs
and their benefits to ELLs, the programs are not without their
critics ranging from misunderstandings and personal attitudes to
political views of language. There are many misunderstandings
about the functions and goals of bilingual programs by teachers,
administrators, and even parents. Therefore, many generalist
teachers, colleagues of bilingual educators, and administrators do

not understand the instructional set-up or curriculum of bilingual classrooms (Samway & McKeon, 1999). Many administrators find themselves overseeing bilingual programs they do not personally understand or agree with philosophically. Without a firm foundation of knowledge and research about the functions and purposes of a well-implemented bilingual education program by both teachers and administrators, the parents of ELLs find themselves confused about the appropriate educational placement for their children when English is not the student's first language or even a language spoken at home (Robles-Goodwin, Mohr, Wilhelm, & Contreras, 2005). With that reality, many parents choose to waive the right to enroll their children in bilingual programs because of the misunderstandings they have about the program (Robles-Goodwin, 2004). Usually there is not a professional educator on staff to present the options and benefits of bilingual education. In fact, when you ask most parents why they chose for their child not to be in a bilingual program, they say "because I want my child to learn English" or "I do not want my child to be in a remedial program." Both of these responses indicate their misunderstandings about a program that should not be compensatory or delay the acquisition of English (Robles-Goodwin, 2004). With this scenario, most of the ELLs that could be best served in a bilingual program will be found in "regular" classrooms, not bilingual classes. The sink-or-swim analogy is often used to describe bilingual children in mainstream classrooms because many of them "swim" and stay afloat with their studies without first language support found in bilingual programs, but many more have sunk because they could not survive (Rodríguez, Ramos, & Ruiz-Escalante, 1994). They usually continue to fall behind in their studies until many reach a point in which they may choose to drop out of school because they can see no way of ever catching up with their peers. Even though ELLs make some progress, they are still lagging behind the mainstream students who also made progress during the year (Samway & McKeon, 1999; Ovando & Collier, 1998).

English as a second language programs

In many cases, ELLs in U. S. school districts are assigned to school-wide ESL teachers who typically pull students out of regular classroom instruction for short periods of time with the goal of developing their language proficiencies in English. The ESL instructional time is often focused on teaching simple, repetitive, low-level, and drill-like English skills in listening, speaking, reading, and writing at the student's English proficiency level of beginner, intermediate or advanced (Ovando & Collier, 1998). However, if the ESL teacher does not have a strong background in reading, the reciprocity of reading and writing at high levels can be nominal to nonexistent, with most of the short instructional time being devoted to basic listening and speaking activities and transitional activities (Gibbons, 2002). Although the intent of the ESL instruction is to help students become competent in the English language, the removal from the regular classroom during critical literacy times such as language arts can usually do more harm than good in the long run. In fact, many ESL students are pulled into a class where lower-level cognitive functions are emphasized as opposed to being challenged to think critically at high levels. If this configuration is used, the ELLs may be better served by remaining in the mainstream classroom during language arts (Slavin & Calderon, 2001).

Many educators and administrators believe that students just simply need to learn to speak English. However, there are many English-speaking students that are not academically successful, even though they speak English. To illustrate this point, I once had a very bright student, "Charlie," in my bilingual kindergarten classroom that came to school speaking only Spanish. That year I was fortunate enough to have a piano in my classroom. Since I played a little, I used the piano and music to teach my children English. We would sing songs in Spanish initially and then in English. Charlie loved music and learned a lot of English words through listening and singing. Many times, he would hear a song in English and memorize it, without really understanding all the English words. Since he was fascinated with dinosaurs, he memorized the English words to some dinosaur songs. He would sing, "My name is Stegosaurus. I am a funny looking dinosaur. On my back are many bony plates and on my tail there is more. . ." He listened to these songs many times over and over again in the listening center until he memorized all the words and could sing it in "perfect English." One afternoon while my students were in learning centers, my principal and an area superintendent stopped by unexpectedly to visit my classroom. They wanted to see how the students were coming along with their English development. They stated they did not want to disturb my afternoon routine, and that I should continue as usual. The superintendent walked to the science center where Charlie was making dinosaurs using modeling clay and placing them in their natural habitats. She approached Charlie and said, "Hi." Charlie looked up and said,

"Hi!" "How are you?" asked the superintendent. "I am fine. Thank you. How are you?" responded Charlie. This greeting was a routine or drill we had practiced in English since the beginning of school and what is referred to as Basic Interpersonal Communication Skills (BICS) or survival English. She looked impressed at his remarkable progress in English in such a short time. She then pointed to one of his dinosaurs and asked, "Who is that?" Charlie responded, "A dinosaur." She asked, "What is its name?" As I nervously observed their interaction, I was amazed when Charlie confidently looked up at her and responded, "My name is Stegosaurus. I am a funny looking dinosaur. For on my back are many bony plates and on my tail there is more. . ." He went on until he had recited the entire song using dinosaur facts! Now, I did not tell her what Charlie had just done—memorized a song—especially when she looked at me with an expression of amazement as to my "gift" of teaching English to Spanish-speaking children. I just returned her smile. Now, I could have had another experience if the superintendent had asked Charlie a series of high-level questions such as: If you could be any dinosaur, which one would you choose? Why? These types of questions require a student to reflect critically on the questions and to respond accordingly by using appropriate English vocabulary. However, she had only asked Charlie basic low-level language questions that merely required basic knowledge and memory of English proficiency in listening and speaking. Charlie's basic English knowledge does not ensure his academic success. It is a myth to believe that ELLs only need to learn to speak English to be successful (Samway & McKeon, 1999). After all, there are many students who speak only English and may be failing academically.

The challenge is to balance language learning, literacy, and high levels of critical thinking. Without deliberate and strategic support, many ESL teachers are expected to perform linguistic and literacy miracles in the short ESL instructional times that usually range from 45 minutes to an hour daily. With this instructional pull out approach, many regular classroom teachers do not see themselves as primarily responsible for the academic progress of ELLs, especially since ELLs are pulled out of their classes for ESL instruction. As a result, teachers lower their expectations for student achievement because they begin to think that it is someone else's job to teach "these" students (Mohr, 2004).

English language acquisition and development

Many preservice, beginning, and current teachers and administrators who have not had specialized training for working with diverse cultures or with ELLs, have many questions about what to expect linguistically when they have students in their class who do not speak English and about best educational practices for serving them (Ladson-Billings, 2001). It is important to sort out the myths and realities of language learning as it relates to students learning English as a second language. A teacher's perceptions, values, beliefs, and attitudes about language learning influences students' successes or failures in school. First, learning a second language takes time. Cummins (1981) states it takes approximately 2 to 3 years to learn basic English and approximately 5 to 7 years to learn high-level academic language needed to pass state-level or standardized tests. Many teachers and administrators erroneously believe that "just learning to speak English" at its basic level is sufficient for academic success or placing an ELL in a classroom without any first-language support. When working with young children, it is important to recognize that not only are they learning English, but they are also learning their own first language. Therefore, bilingual teachers will use the Spanish language for the purposes of teaching English (Freeman & Freeman, 1996), and ESL teachers will use many visuals to teach vocabulary. ELL teachers use the known (student's first language) to teach the unknown (English). While many teachers may not agree with this framework, it can be looked at from a different perspective. For example, if a teacher speaking only English wanted to learn to speak Chinese, she could learn Chinese more quickly and efficiently if it is learned through English instead of being totally immersed in a Chinese class with the teacher only speaking Chinese day after day. When learning and using two languages simultaneously, young children may use both languages and code-switch when speaking. When this occurs, they may mix their first and second language within a sentence such as: "Voy a ir a la store when I get home." (I am going to the store when I get home). This example illustrates the processing of two languages at the same time. It should be noted that this process is done automatically or without much thought (Baker, 1996). Many teachers would often believe that a student observed to code-switch was evidence of a lack of command of either language. This linguistic occurrence has now been identified as a high level cognitive function many ELLs use in their thinking and speaking (Berzins & Lopez, 2001).

Many teachers believe young children learn a second language faster than older learners. In reality, while young language learners may learn to speak a new language with little or no accent, older language learners are often more efficient learners because they usually already have a language framework from which to build a new language. They are able to transfer existing knowledge in one language to another one. In other words, an older student may already know how to add and subtract in their language (Ovando & Collier, 1998; Samway & McKeon, 1999). Therefore, for students learning English as a second language, the teacher does not have to "start from the beginning linguistically" and reteach the skills of adding and subtracting. The teacher only needs to teach the English vocabulary words associated with the skills.

Therefore, some myths that need to be debunked in terms of learning English are:

- Learning to speak English is a fast process. In fact, it is not. Learning English *takes time*.

- Speaking the first language at home will delay the learning of English at school. In fact, students speaking their first language at home *will not confuse or slow down* the English language learning process.

- Learning English needs to occur from the "beginning" no matter what is known in the first language. In fact, older learners *will transfer* their knowledge in their first language to English. The learner *does not have to start from the beginning* to learn English.

- Acquiring English follows a different pattern from that used to learn the first language. In fact, *it follows a similar pattern*. It goes through developmental stages much like first language patterns (Krashen, 1999; Samway & McKeon, 1999).

Teachers may ask themselves: What should I expect from students learning English? As stated before, learning English takes much time and practice. Many teachers of ELLs may not have the same high expectations for ELLs. Teachers with good intentions can operate from two perspectives when working with ELLs that do not speak or participate in English. One stance is that ELLs who do not speak English at home do not need to have good self-esteem at school while learning English. Another view is what Berzins and Lopez (2001) describe as the "pobrecito" (poor little one) framework of teachers making excuses for why the student cannot learn. While both of these approaches would seemingly appear to reflect an appropriate and culturally responsive approach to working with ELLs, it demonstrates a mindset of not expecting much from the ELL student and delivering academically inferior instruction (Ladson-Billings, 2001). A student may go through a "silent period" in which they may not say a word. During this time, it is important for teachers to allow ample wait time for students to process information in two languages (Samway & McKeon, 1999). Sufficient wait time of 4-7 seconds should be given when asking ELLs to respond to a verbal question. If a student does not respond after the wait time, the teacher can ask the student to continue thinking about the response and that she will get back with them. This practice signals to the student that the teacher understands the language acquisition process and has high expectations for all students (Diaz & Flores, 2001). The silent period can last as long as six months for some students. During this time, their reading and writing skills may develop before the speaking skills. The teacher should expect for the learning to transfer from the first language to English (Krashen, 1987; Tabors, 1997). As students learn English, they will process through two stages of language learning. Basic Interpersonal Communication Skills (BICS) sometimes referred to as "social or playground" language takes usually 2-3 years to develop. Advanced language levels referred to as Cognitive Academic Language Proficiency (CALP) takes approximately 5 to 7 years to develop (Cummins, 1981). This high level of language development is needed for students to think creatively and abstractly about language. Teachers of ELLs need to keep in mind the students need advanced language levels to do well on achievement tests.

What are some best practices for ELLs?

What should teachers do if they have ELLs in their classes?
- *Teachers should speak slowly and clearly—simplify language.* Some teachers talk loudly when students appear not to understand. However, speaking loudly will not help them understand any better.
- *Teachers may need to repeat or paraphrase directions several times or even model with actions.* Effective teachers make students feel comfortable learning English. They lower the student's affective filter or learning frustrations when learning a new language.
- *The teachers should create an environment in which students feel safe to take linguistic risks.*

- Most importantly, *teachers must always have high expectations for learning by providing many different types of learning experiences with appropriate support* (Diaz & Flores, 2001).
- They need to make learning understandable, which is often referred to as comprehensible input (CI). *They make learning meaningful by validating the language, culture and experiences the students bring to school and incorporate them into the curriculum.*

Effective teachers use literature and a variety of books to provide CI and to depict aspects of the student's culture (Krashen, 1987). Books provide a platform for developing many different aspects of literacy. Big books and reading aloud can provide opportunities to engage students in a motivating way (Herrell, 2000). Books can be used to present informational and appropriate vocabulary for a variety of interests and themes. They can be used to expose ELLs to the English language structures, patterns, and discourse. The read alouds can be expanded to motivate students, especially bilingual students, to join their voices to put on play, choral reading, and recitation of a favorite poem/song/game:

Los elefantes (Spanish)	The Elephant Song
Un elefante se balanceaba	One elephant went out to play
sobre la tela de una araña.	Out on a spider's web one day.
Como veía que resistía.	He had such enormous fun.
Fue a llamar a otro elefante.	He called another elephant to play.
Dos elefantes. . .	Two elephants. . .

Tres elefantes. . .   Three elephants. . .

This counting song can be played as a game. While the group stands in a circle and sing, one child makes the slow-motion sway walk of an elephant inside the circle. At the end of the first verse, the child picks a second child, and both do the slow motion elephant sway walk, and so on (Orozco, 1994). There are many variations of this song throughout Latin America.

Readers' theatre is usually characterized by the transformation of a story into a play. Writing the scripts involves many literacy processes and negotiations among students about their interpretations of the text. These conversations occur in social interactions as students read various texts and discuss the roles of the presentation in terms of what parts should be added, deleted, or refined for the performance. These types of activities demonstrate engaging and motivational contexts that are particularly appropriate for students learning English. McCauley and McCauley (1992) found that the repeated reading of text through choral reading allowed ELLs to use English in a no-risk environment, allowing them to mispronounce English words that could easily be absorbed by the overriding voices of the group. ELLs can usually understand more language than they can produce. By understanding the Vygotskian concept of language mediating thinking, teachers should include a variety of cognitive activities such as problem-solving; creating; reasoning; recognizing similarities and differences; understanding relationships; sorting sounds, letters, words, and ideas into categories or groups; recalling events, ideas; and using language to speak, write, and read with appropriate language scaffolding (Gibbons, 2002).

Language and literacy activities for ELLs should include but not be limited to interactive journal writing, letter writing/pen pals, Drop Everything and Read (D.E.A.R) time, language experiences, storytelling and retelling, daily news, writing text for wordless picture books, reading predictable books, shared reading, story listening, poetry, songs, chants, message boards, music, art, drama, and Reader's Theater (Freeman & Freeman, 2000). Some poetry books include *A light in the attic* (Silverstein, 1981), *Falling up* (Silverstein, 1996), *A pizza the size of the sun* (Prelutsky, 1996), and *Something big has been here* (Prelutsky, 1990). Some books that have a repeated pattern of some type that can be used include *Mary wore her red dress and Henry wore his green sneakers* (Peek, 1985) and *Brown bear, Brown bear,* (Martin, 1967). For familiar cultural sequences such as cardinal and ordinal numbers, *Feast for Ten* (Falwell, 1993), *Just a minute* (Morales, 2003), and *Chicken soup with rice* (Sendak, 1962) are good resources.

Building English vocabulary is an important ingredient in learning to read fluently and in being able to learn and understand complex concepts. Large vocabulary knowledge facilitates reading comprehension and makes learning to read new ideas and concepts possible (Meire, 2004).

There should be daily activities that strengthen ELLs' cognitive development because it is closely tied to the development of language and literacy (Opitz & Rasinski, 1998). Some literacy examples include:

- developing problem-solving skills and creativity;

- building skills that help them recognize differences and similarities;
- helping them see relationships between and among ideas, words, and objects;
- building their memory and recall for events, people and ideas; and
- developing the ability to sequence ideas and events.

Higher order mental tasks, the ability to reason, and abstract reasoning require intensive and deliberate instruction. There should be a variety of language and literacy activities that lay the foundations needed to be a successful reader and writer (Meier, 2004).

Heath (1989) stated, ". . . for all children, academic success depends less on the specific language they speak than on the ways of using the language they know" (p. 144). Clay (1993) believed that the least complicated entry to literacy was to use the language the children already know and speak because it can be used to power their literacy learning.

Successful reading strategies research has shown that reading comprehension is a constructive process where students construct meaning by interacting with the text. The interaction involves the student's prior knowledge, the text, and the reading context (Cooper, 2003; Herrell, 2000). Expert readers have strategies or plans to help them solve problems and construct meaning before, during, and after reading. Successful reading transfer strategies include constructing meaning by helping students visualize or making pictures in their heads as they read. This strategy is sometimes referred to as mental imaging, which enhances understanding (Cooper, 2003).

Language and literacy should occur all day long. Teachers are encouraged to read aloud to ELLs for 20-30 minutes per day, in an interactive way. This sharing is an avenue for building the many language and reading foundations needed to accelerate English language skills. These activities provide perfect opportunities to expand cognitive, language, and memory skills (Opitz & Rasinski, 1998).

How can I work with the families of my ELLs?

- Schedule regular meetings with parents in which language and literacy development are discussed.
- Be flexible with the place and time of the meetings in order to accommodate working parents, transportation issues, and childcare.
- If feasible, make certain to provide an interpreter for the meeting.
- Include provisions for childcare in case children are brought to the meeting.
- Have informal conversations with parents in order to learn about their children from their point of view. They can contribute valuable information regarding their children's strengths and unique needs.
- There are many benefits to having the teacher make home visits to learn more about the family and the home environment of students.

The teacher can use the experience to prepare and provide a culturally responsive curriculum structure at school (Hildebrand, Phenice, Gray, & Hines, 2000). For example, I once had an ELL I felt was not "with it." As a teacher, it annoyed me when students seemed irresponsible when it came to school and learning. He would often fall asleep during the day. I scheduled a home visit and was surprised to discover multiple families living in a small apartment. The adults living in the apartment had different working schedules ranging from morning to night. As a result, this student experienced many challenges at home from a student perspective. He did not have a quiet place to do his homework other than a small area in a closet. The television was on all day and night, and he did not have a regular bedtime schedule allowing him to sleep in a noiseless environment. After my home visit, I was more compassionate about the daily struggles usually taken for granted by many middle-class values and experiences. As a result, I made instructional adjustments that allowed the student to begin his homework at school.

Many cultures value and respect the role of teachers; therefore, many parents will not dispute or disagree with a teacher's recommendation regarding how best to help their children learn English (Robles-Goodwin, 2004). Many teachers often ill advise parents with limited English levels to only speak English at home with their children. If this is the case, ELLs will only be exposed to fragmented English at home. While teachers may believe this recommendation to parents will help ELLs learn English rapidly, it has very harmful effects. Since most young ELLs are learning their own language, as well as learning English at school, parents should be encouraged to speak their first or "better" language with their children. Otherwise, ELLs may only develop minimal literacy skills in their first language and English.

What's next? The promises for the future

Accelerating the English proficiency of ELLs is a multifaceted effort by many people including educators, administrators, and parents. Making appropriate decisions regarding the best educational practices and programs to implement necessitates knowing how ELLs acquire English and the challenges involved. Teachers must use proven best instructional strategies to teach ELLs in engaging and meaningful ways. ESL instruction needs to include a combination of best practices that utilize proven research-based literacy strategies (McGee & Richgels, 1996) . The mainstream and ESL teacher are encouraged to accept responsibility for ELLs and to work together to make appropriate teaching modifications that include explicit teaching of the English language system, increase vocabulary knowledge, and make meaningful connections to real-life situations. To reiterate some strategies for working with ELLs:

Simplify your language.
  - Avoid slang expressions.
  - Rephrase instead of repeating.
  - Speak in a normal tone.

Demonstrate and use manipulatives
  - Use gestures and facial expressions.
  - Use pictures and real objects to teach vocabulary.

Adapt instruction
  - Use pictures, charts, time lines, and diagrams.
  - Make information comprehensible and meaningful (relevant to the culture).

Group students
- Use cooperative grouping for peer interaction and language development.
- Group students according to their language level for attaining higher language levels among the group.

Increase wait time
- Allow students time to process information for answering questions in English.

Implications

Educators must have high educational expectations for all ELLs. After all, efforts must be doubled or even tripled to serve the students who need them the most. Students excel when learning in an enriched environment where they have choices for the way they demonstrate mastery. Effective instruction should be designed to appeal to the variety of diverse learners prevalent in today's classrooms (Ladson-Billings, 2001). ELLs deserve to have teachers and systems willing to go beyond using traditional practices and beliefs and strive to implement culturally responsive instruction in a respectful way in order to fulfill the promises of an equitable education to our future generations.

References

August, D., & Hakuta, K. (1997). *Improving schooling for language-minority children*. Washington, DC: National Academy Press.

Baker, C. (1996). *Foundations of bilingual education and bilingualism*. Bristol, PA: Multilingual Matters Ltd.

Berzins, M. E., & Lopez. A. E. (2001). Starting off right: Planting the seeds for biliteracy. In M. Reyes & J. Halcon (Eds.), *The best for our children: Critical perspectives in literacy for Latino students* (pp. 81-95). New York: Teachers College Press.

Clay, M. (1993). *An observation survey of early literacy achievement*. Portsmouth, NH: Heinemann.

Cole, R. W. (Ed.) (1995). *Educating everybody's children: Diverse teaching strategies for diverse learners*. Alexandria, VA: Association for the Supervision and Curriculum Development.

Collier, V. P. (1987). Age and acquisition of second language for academic purposes. *TESOL Quarterly, 21*, 617-641.

Cooper, J. D. (2003). *Literacy: Helping children construct meaning*. Boston: Houghton Mifflin Company.

Crawford, J. (1991). *Bilingual education: History, politics, theory, and practice*. Los Angeles: Bilingual Educational Services, Inc.

Cummins, J. (1981). The role of primary language development in promoting educational success for language minority students. In *California State Department of Education, Schooling and language minority students: A theoretical framework* (pp. 3-49). Los Angeles: National Evaluation, Dissemination, and Assessment Center, California State University, Los Angeles.

de la Luz Reyes, M. (2001). Unleashing possibilities: Biliteracy in the primary grades. In M. Reyes & J. Halcon (Eds.), *The best for our children: Critical perspectives in literacy for Latino students* (pp. 29-47). New York: Teachers College Press.

Diaz, E., & Flores, B. (2001). Teachers as sociocultural, sociohistorical mediator: Teaching to the potential. In M. Reyes & J. Halcon (Eds.), *The best for our children: Critical perspectives in literacy for Latino students* (pp. 29-47). New York: Teachers College Press.

Espinoza-Herold, M. (2003). *Issues in Latino education: Race, school culture, and the politics of academic success.* Boston: Pearson Education Group, Inc.

Falwell, C. (1993). *Feast for 10.* Boston: Houghton Mifflin.

Freeman, D. E., & Freeman, Y. S. (1993). Strategies for promoting the primary Languages of all students. *The Reading Teacher, 46,* 552-558.

Freeman, Y. S., & Freeman, D. E. (1996). *Teaching reading and writing in Spanish in the bilingual classroom.* Portsmouth, NH: Heinemann.

Freeman, D. E., & Freeman, Y. S. (2000). *Teaching reading in multilingual classrooms.* Portsmouth, NH: Heinemann.

Gay, G. (2000). *Culturally responsive teaching: Theory, research, & practice.* New York: Teachers College Press.

Gibbons, P. (2002). *Scaffolding language, scaffolding learning: Teaching second language learners in the mainstream classroom.* Portsmouth, NH: Heinemann.

Heath, S. B. (1989). Sociocultural contexts of language development. In *Beyond language: Social and cultural factors in schooling language minority students.* Los Angeles: California State University; Evaluation, Dissemination and Assessment Center.

Herrell, A. L. (2000). *Fifty strategies for teaching English language learners.* Upper Saddle River, NJ: Prentice-Hall, Inc.

Hilderbrand, V., Phenice, L. A., Gray, M. M., & Hines, R. P. (2000). *Knowing and serving diverse families.* Upper Saddle River, NJ: Prentice-Hall, Inc.

Jiménez, R. T., García, G. E., & Pearson, P. D. (1996). The reading strategies of bilingual Latina/o students who are successful English readers: Opportunities and obstacles. *Reading Research Quarterly, 31*, 91-112.

Krashen, S. D. (1981). Bilingual education and second language acquisition theory. In *Schooling and language minority students: A theoretical framework* (pp. 3-49). Los Angeles, CA: National Evaluation, Dissemination, and Assessment Center, California State University, Los Angeles.

Krashen, S. D. (1987). *Principles and practice in second language acquisition.* New York: Prentice Hall.

Krashen, S. D. (1999). *Condemned without a trial: Bogus arguments against bilingual education.* Portsmouth, NH: Heinemann.

Ladson-Billings, G. (1994). *The dreamkeepers: Successful teachers for African-American children.* San Francisco: Jossey-Bass.

Ladson-Billings, G. (2001). *Crossing over to Canaan: The journey of new teachers in diverse classrooms.* San Francisco: John Wiley & Sons, Inc.

Lindholm-Leary, K. (2000). *Biliteracy for a global society: An idea book on dual language education.* Washington, DC: National Clearinghouse for Bilingual Education.

McCandless, E., Rossi, R., & Daugherty, S. (1996). *Are limited English proficient (LEP) students being taught by teachers with LEP training?* Washington, DC: U. S. Department of Education, National Center for Education Statistics (NCES 97-907).

McCauley, J. K., & McCauley, D. S. (1992). Using choral reading to promote language learning for ESL students. *The Reading Teacher, 45*, 526-533.

McGee, L. M. & Richgels, D. J. (1996). *Literacy's beginnings: Supporting young readers and writers.* Boston: Allyn and Bacon.

Meier, D. R, (2004). *The young child's memory for words: Developing first and second language literacy.* New York: Teachers College Press.

Mohr, K. A. J. (2004). English as an accelerated language: A call to action for reading teachers. *The Reading Teacher, 58*(1), 18-26.

Morales, Y. (2003). *Just a minute: A trickster tale and counting book.* San Francisco: Chronicle Books.

Opitz, M. F., & Rasinski, T. V. (1998). *Good-bye round robin: Twenty-five oral reading strategies.* Portsmouth, NH: Heinemann.

Orozco, J. (1994). *De colores: And other Latin-American folk songs for children.* New York: Dutton Children's Books.

Ovando, C. J. & Collier, V. P. (1998). *Bilingual and ESL classrooms: Teaching in multicultural contexts.* Boston: The McGraw-Hill Companies, Inc.

Peek, M. (1985). *Mary wore her red dress and Henry wore his green sneakers.* New York: Clarion.

Prelutsky, J. (1996). *A pizza the size of the sun.* New York: Scholastic.

Prelutsky, J. (1990). *Something big has been here.* New York: Greenwillow Books.

Robles-Goodwin, P. J. (2004, December). *Leave no parent behind . . .: An investigation into the educational perceptions of Latino parents with young children in urban, suburban, and rural school settings.* Paper presented at the meeting of the Hawaii International Conference on Education in Honolulu.

Robles-Goodwin, P. J., Mohr, K. A. J., Wilhelm, R. W., & Contreras, G. (2005, May). *Fronteras y barreras: Una investigación de los desafíos educativos para el niño migrante. (Borders and barriers: An investigation of the educational challenges for Mexican immigrant children).* Paper presented at the meeting of The Canadian Anthropological Society (CASCA) & the Society for the

Anthropology of North America (SANA) & Facultad de Ciencias Antropológicas de la Universidad Autonoma de Yucatán (UADY), Mérida, México.

Rodríguez, R., Ramos, N. J. & Ruiz-Escalante, J. A. (Eds.). (1994). *Compendium of readings in bilingual education: Issues and practices.* Texas Association for Bilingual Education.

Samway, K. D., & McKeon, D. (1999). *Myths and realities: Best practices for Language minority students.* Portsmouth, NH: Heinemann.

Sendak, M. (1962). *Chicken soup with rice.* New York: Scholastic Inc.

Silverstein, S. (1981). *A light in the attic.* New York: Harper & Row.

Silverstein, S. (1996). *Falling up: Poems and drawings.* New York: HarperCollins.

Slavin, R. E., & Calderon, M. (Eds.). (2001). *Effective programs for Latino students.* Mahway, NJ: Erlbaum.

Tabors, P. O. (1997). *One child, two languages: A guide for preschool educators of children learning English as a second language.* Baltimore: Paul H. Brookes Publishing Company.

Tinajero, J. V., & Devillar, R. A. (Eds.). (2000). *The power of two languages 2000: Effective dual-language use across the curriculum.* New York: McGraw-Hill School Division.

Closing the Achievement Gap for English Language Learners: Addressing Linguistic, Cultural and Educational Needs in In-School and After-School Programs

Eva Midobuche and Alfredo Benavides
Texas Tech University

One of our English as a Second Language (ESL) preservice teachers, who has just finished her student teaching, recently walked into our office with a very important incident to report to us. She was visibly shaken as she recalled the incident. She had completed her student teaching in two different grade levels and was very concerned about her seventh grade placement. Towards the end of her student teaching semester she discovered that a new Hispanic student had been recently enrolled and placed into her cooperating teacher's classroom. Upon entering the classroom she saw the new student sitting by herself at the back of the room. She approached and began to ask questions in order to elicit some information. The questions were simple, including name, age, and former school. They were designed to establish the student's identity. The student could not respond in English. Our student teacher was initially surprised. However, in her limited Spanish she began to ask the student more questions.

It was at this point that the cooperating teacher informed her that she should not worry about this particular student. The teacher indicated that the new student would merely be allowed to sit in the back of the classroom by herself. Concerned, the ESL student teacher asked if she could adapt materials for the student. The teacher again told the student teacher not to worry. The immigrant student continued to sit in the back of the room without anyone attempting to instruct her while other students (including those who were Hispanic) made fun of her. There was no attempt by the teacher to correct this behavior. Our student teacher was completely shocked by what she had witnessed and reported the incident.

Unfortunately, the situation described is not an isolated incident. These types of situations are occurring in many of our classrooms across the country. In this particular case the student teacher reported the situation. She did so because of her preparation as a future teacher, her courage, and ultimately her strong commitment to educating English Language Learners (ELLs) (Midobuche, Benavides, & Díaz, 2006). Midobuche (1999, 2001a; 2001b) stresses that there exists a great need in education for all of our teachers to educate every student who comes through their doors. A teacher should not only respect students, but also be aware of cultural and linguistic differences (Midobuche, 1999).

In an ethnographic study conducted in a bilingual and dual language setting Díaz (2001) found that a lack of literature exists in the education of Mexican immigrant middle school students. After studying seven recent middle school immigrant students for two years and using a triangulation method of research analysis, she found that bilingual education teachers in her sample lacked:

- preparation in bilingual education;
- second language acquisition theory and cultural knowledge;
- knowledge of pedagogy;
- teacher to student communication strategies;
- knowledge of heritage language use;

- strategies for validating the students' heritage; and,
- strategies for parental communication and involvement.

In her conclusions Díaz reported that bilingual teachers did not get to know their immigrant students and although they spoke Spanish, they deferred to their English-speaking students to do the translating for the ELLs and did not provide adequate time for these translations. Díaz found that the bilingual education teachers in her study were making a 'conscious' decision not to validate the immigrant students' heritage language and culture. Díaz also found that immigrant parents were making great efforts to spend time with their children, and that they were concerned about their children not learning English. Parents frequently expressed the sentiment that they wanted to return to Mexico because of the challenges of transitioning into the United States. The students in this study often felt isolated even from other immigrant students who had lived in the United States for a longer period of time. The following short story is a prime example of the students in Díaz' study.

> Pedro is a dedicated worker as he works long hours every weekend to help his parents with living expenses. He tells his sister, who is worried about many things—only one of which is family finances—that he will also help her financially when he grows up. He tells her to ask God to let him become an adult soon, in order for this to happen, for him to be able to give her money. One of his journal entries described this wish eloquently.

El Día del Lanto y Dolor

Ayer miré llorar a mi mamá y me dolió mucho porque ella ha sufrido mucho por mi y mi hermano. La abrazé y le dije que le pida a Dios que crezca pronto para poder seguir adelante y

*para que ella ya no se preocupara por nada.
Entonces recordé las Navidades con la familia que
vivíamos porque no teníamos casa. Todos habrían regalos
menos nosotros y nos sacaban para fuera. Y mi hermana se iba
a una tienda a barrer para traernos algo de comer. Ayer le dije
a ella que yo recordaba todo y muchas cosas más y que estaba
orgulloso porque estamos ahora en Phoenix. Y yo sé que vamos
a ser felices. Le di gracias por demostrarnos tanto amor y lloré
mucho escondido porque ella no merece sufrir.*

The Day of Weeping and Deep Pain

Yesterday I saw my mother crying and it hurt me very much
because she has suffered very much for me and for my brother.
I hugged her and I asked her to ask God to enable me to
become an adult so I could accomplish my goals and so she
wouldn't have to worry about anything. I remembered the
Christmas times with the family we lived with. We didn't have
our own house. Everyone would open their gifts except our
family and they would ask us to leave. My sister would work
cleaning a store, to give us money to eat. I told her that I
remembered everything she has done for us and much more and
that I was proud because we were now in Phoenix. I know we
are going to be happy. I thanked her for demonstrating her love
to us and I cried a lot because she doesn't deserve to suffer. I
didn't let anyone see me cry (Díaz, 2001, pp. 101-102).

Pedro's seventh grade emotions and thought processes are
captured here in a very uninhibited manner. His journal entries
demonstrate mature and considered thinking beyond himself. In
the classroom, Pedro's attempts at 'schooling' are stifled by
seemingly uncaring teachers. In his efforts to better understand a
science lesson, Pedro asked a question in Spanish and was told by
his 'bilingual' science teacher, "Speak English please." And Pedro
is not alone. All students in the same science class are often given

'choices' as to what grade they want to earn. The teacher gives each student a sheet, written only in English, describing which assignments will be required for each grade. The students have a grade choice between an "A," "B," or "C." However, the "C" category requires the most assignments, and requires students to earn the most points—all this in order to "earn" the lowest grade possible. However, what makes the "C" so attractive is the fact that one of the assignments in this category can be done "in a language other than English." Students like Pedro jump at the opportunity to demonstrate what they know in their own native language (Díaz, 2001).

Many factors will affect classroom performance of future teachers across the nation but none more critically than the presence of children whose first language is not English. High stakes testing, No Child Left Behind legislation, the challenges presented by a linguistically and culturally diverse population, and high numbers of English Language Learners have combined to make many teachers and schools take notice of how inadequately prepared they are to handle linguistic and cultural diversity in their classrooms. While bilingual education and English as a Second Language teachers should have the academic preparation necessary to teach in bilingual education and ESL classrooms across our nation, the number of bilingual and ESL teachers needed to keep up with the growing demand will probably never be realized.

According to Boe (1990), the shortage of bilingual educators has been well documented since the early 1980's. Boe noted at the time, that no national database of bilingual education teachers was available to support refined supply and demand research in this area. This shortage was referred to by Gold (1992), as "the single

greatest barrier to the improvement of instructional programs for
LEP students" (p. 223). Furthermore, the lack of a bilingual
teacher supply is supported in studies by Gándara (1986), Macías
(1989), Quezada (1991), Torres-Guzman and Goodwin (1995),
Crawford (1997), Menken and Holmes (2000), and Menken and
Antunez (2001).

More recently, the difficulty in finding and attracting teachers
for bilingual classrooms was pointed out by Abdelrahim (August,
2005). Abdelrahim noted that huge efforts need to be made in
order to recruit more minority teachers, especially teachers
prepared to work with students from diverse linguistic and cultural
backgrounds. In a second report, Abdelrahim (February, 2005),
points out that schools will need to hire as many as two million
new teachers in the coming decade. She notes that this great
teacher shortage will be particularly crucial in the areas of
bilingual and ESL education.

Moss and Puma (1995) stated that the inadequate supply of
bilingual teachers had forced many districts to hire and therefore
rely on uncertified aides, whose only qualification in many cases
was the ability to speak another language. They also reported that
in 1991-1992 nearly three out of five ELLs in high-poverty schools
nationwide were taught English reading by these paraprofessionals,
most of whom had no education beyond high school.

Abdelrahim (2005) suggested that hiring teachers from abroad
might alleviate the critical teacher shortage in bilingual education.
Barbe (2006) reports that because of a shortage of bilingual
education teachers in the Jacksonville (Texas) Independent School
District, administrators made a recruiting trip to Monterrey,
Mexico to recruit Mexican teachers. They eventually brought

seven teachers from Mexico. This trip was funded by the Texas Education Agency and facilitated by the Region 4 Service Center.

In a related situation, the Associated Press (2006) reported that Dallas Independent School District officials wanted to work with other urban school systems to initiate changes in the current immigration laws in order to permit them to hire college-educated illegal immigrants to address the growing shortage of bilingual teachers in their district. This request is in conflict with current U.S. immigration law. However, due to the great need for these teachers, Dallas school officials are seeking a means to modify the law.

It is apparent to many educators that there is a shortage of bilingual and ESL teachers. Therefore, because of this shortage, many ELLs will eventually need to be placed in regular classrooms with mainstream teachers. The convergence of this shortage and other factors has created a need to carefully examine what bilingual education, ESL, and mainstream teachers need to know about meeting the needs of ELLs. These needs will affect how best practices are incorporated into everyday classrooms across our educational landscape.

According to Murdock (2002), the Texas population will become larger, older, and increasingly more diverse in the next few decades. In his 'fast-growth' scenario Murdock predicts that Texas will add 29.7 million people by the year 2040. Under this scenario the State's population would be 24.2% European American, 7.9% African American, 59.1% Hispanic, and 8.8% members of other racial/ethnic groups. What should be of concern to Texas educators is how the Texas education system will respond to this population shift. Recently Texas Hispanic schoolchildren became

the majority in Texas schools. According to the Texas Education
Agency's Academic Excellence Indicator System (AEIS) Report
for 2005, Hispanic children numbered 1,961,549 compared to
1,653,008 European American children.

Both of these reports should prompt all Texas educators to
address the specific linguistic, cultural, and educational needs of
Hispanic students. While Hispanic K-12 students, many of whom
are ELLs, have already become the majority in Texas, the Texas
Education Agency (2005) reports that the number of Hispanic
teachers in Texas is only 19.5% of the teaching force. The Texas
Education Agency also reports that the number of identified ELLs
in Texas has grown to 684,007. While this number is 52,473 larger
than the number of children identified as actually enrolled in
Bilingual and ESL education, it still represents a large issue for
educators because there are only 24,790 Bilingual and ESL
teachers in the entire state—or only 8.4% of all teachers (Texas
Education Agency, 2005).   As the numbers of ELLs continue to
grow, meeting their educational needs will become a greater issue
for all Texas educators.

At the national level, the National Clearinghouse for English
Language Acquisition (NCELA) reports that during the 2003-2004
school year, there were 5,014,437 children who are English
Language Learners in the United States. Although gathering
accurate data on ELLs is often difficult, the national growth of this
particular segment of the school-age population has been very
rapid. However, many teachers are unprepared to teach these
students in their classrooms. The U.S. Department of Education
National Center for Education Statistics (NCES 2002), points out
that while many teachers report having had ELLs in their

classrooms, the number of teachers who have had at least 8 or more hours of training in the past three years on how to teach these students was very low. For example, according to this NCES Report, 55.7 % of Texas teachers reported that they had ELLs in their classrooms, yet only 17.9% had at least the 8 hours of formal preparation. Other states reported a similar pattern. Selected examples from the National Center for Education Statistics Report (2002) are as follows:

State	% of Teachers Who Taught ELLs	% with 8 or more hours of formal preparation
Arizona	67.8%	23.2%
Colorado	53.2%	13.2%
Georgia	35.2%	6.2%
Illinois	37.1%	7.1%
Indiana	29.0%	1.9%
New Mexico	64.7%	33.2%
California	75.2%	49.2%
Nevada	67.5%	18.6%
Arkansas	29.9%	12.5%
Louisiana	16.4%	3.1%
Oklahoma	32.9%	5.2%

Institutions of higher education (IHEs) have not helped to solve the problem because they have not offered preservice teachers very much in terms of helping them prepare for teaching ELLs. According to Menken and Antunez (2001), only a small minority of colleges and universities offer a specialized program to prepare bilingual teachers and fewer than 1/6 of the institutions studied required any preparation for mainstream teachers working with ELLs. Menken and Antunez also report that in a survey for the American Association of Colleges of Teacher Education (AACTE), 169 out of 417 institutions (41%) reported requiring coursework on issues regarding ELLs. However, since those institutions with bilingual education and English as a Second Language (ESL) programs were also included in this survey, it is likely that only a small number of these 169 institutions required that mainstream teachers also take coursework for meeting the educational needs of ELLs.

The National Center for English Language Acquisition (2002) also reported that just over 79% or 3,598,451 ELLs in the United States spoke Spanish as their heritage language while the next closest heritage language spoken was Vietnamese with 1.953% or 88,906 Vietnamese-speaking students. In classifying ELLs and their heritage languages, NCELA reported a total of 384 reported languages spoken by ELLs in U.S. schools. These students bring a different set of experiences and perspectives to the classroom. The likelihood that any teacher will one day be teaching ELLs in a classroom is high. Therefore, if teachers have not had experience with ELLs or linguistically diverse learners, it is imperative to understand these students in terms of their linguistic, cultural, and educational needs. Teaching from this perspective is what Villegas and Lucas (2002) refer to as culturally responsive teaching.

Bilingual Education and ESL teacher preparation programs in university Colleges of Education must address those areas that Díaz's study found lacking and emphasize the practices that helped our student teacher to recognize and become responsive to that immigrant student's linguistic, cultural and educational needs. We must ensure that as a minimum, preservice teachers are exposed to and understand the individual state Bilingual Education and ESL standards and competencies. This would be in addition to the TESOL/NCATE Standards for P-12 Teacher Education Programs.

TESOL (Teachers of English to Speakers of Other Languages) (2003) recommends that preservice teachers understand the importance of language in the classroom and should be able to create a language-rich learning environment in order to foster heritage and target language development among ELLs. Also, preservice teachers need to be made aware that students come to the educational environment with previously developed language skills and whenever possible attempt to extend and use the students' heritage language for learning the target language and for learning in other areas.

TESOL also stresses culture. Preservice teachers should know that diversity is an asset and respond positively to it. Teachers need to know that all students can learn when cultural factors are recognized, respected, and accommodated. This could also be integrated into their teaching (TESOL, 2003). Preservice teachers can also plan for multi-level classrooms using standards-based ESL in content curriculum and that these classrooms should also be supportive in positive climates for language learners. Preservice teachers can also serve as professional resources, advocate for ELLs, and build partnerships with the students' families. These professional educators need to have preparation in order to be able to assess ELLs' content area achievement independently from their language ability and adapt materials at varying stages of language development (TESOL, 2003).

All standards for teaching are important. These are mentioned merely as examples. It is important to understand that many preservice teachers as well as other mainstream teachers have access to this type of preparation. It is at this critical stage that institutions of higher education must step in to ensure that all teachers receive the type of preparation that will include careful attention to standards and competencies that pinpoint the particular needs of English Language Learners. It is vital for the education community to come to the realization that much remains to be done in addressing the needs of ELLs.

Learning does not occur solely in the classroom. According to Gallego, Rueda, and Moll (2003), "schools may extract valuable lessons by attending to how learning occurs in places outside the traditional classroom" (p. 387). Therefore, there are other approaches that can be used to assist in the education of English Language Learners. Traditional classroom instruction can be supplemented by learning activities outside of the classroom. There are many approaches that can be utilized to add to what teachers are doing in the classroom. The National Association of Elementary School Principals (1993) states that "the time spent by a child outside school and away from parents may be greater than the time spent at school. These hours are too many and too precious to waste" (p. 1). Therefore, developing positive parental involvement is a goal that should be pursued in order to assist in the learning development of ELLs.

Tutoring programs can also be another means of addressing the educational needs of ELLs. In January 2005 the Office for Planning, Grants, and Evaluation from the Texas Education Agency conducted its first evaluation of the 21st Century

Community Learning Centers (CCLC) for projects funded for the 2003 - 2004 school year. Previous research on the effectiveness of after-school programs had been conducted by the U.S. Department of Education (2003), The Harvard Family Research Project (2002), and The National Institute on Out of School Time (2003) and has shown that these programs can have a positive impact on student classroom and out-of-school behavior, and on students' academic performance. The 21st Century Community Learning Centers program of the U.S. Department of Education was honored in 2002 for its partnership with the C.S. Mott Foundation in its efforts to help establish public schools as community learning centers and offer quality after-school programs for children (U.S. Department of Education, 2002). The 21st CCLC Program is a key component of President Bush's No Child Left Behind Act. The focus of the program is to provide expanded academic enrichment for children who attend high-poverty schools, including activities designed to help students meet local and state standards.

In its first state evaluation report of the 21st CCLCs, the Texas Education Agency (2005) found that they focused most of their efforts on providing accelerated instruction and tutorials in basic academic skills--mathematics, reading, and social studies in addition to fine arts and sports activities. These activities were conducted in settings where the vast majority of the teaching staff was certified and where community involvement was present. The report also stated that the CCLCs were providing high-quality instruction with local flexibility and community involvement. Although over 33% of Texas participants in CCLCs are ELLs, more emphasis needs to be placed on addressing the linguistic needs of these particular students. An example of a program addressing these needs is the Lubbock-Cooper 21st CCLC Program. This project encompasses five rural school districts in the Lubbock area. The project has a component directly linked to Texas Tech University's Bilingual Education and Diversity Studies Program in the College of Education. Graduate and undergraduate students specializing in bilingual education form a cadre of tutor-mentors who work with individual districts to assist in providing tutoring in mathematics, science and reading to ELLs in these districts. In addition to meeting the English language needs of the Spanish-speaking ELLs the project also has begun to address the linguistic and cultural needs of a German speaking ELL Mennonite community (Midobuche, Benavides, & Angulo, 2006).

The 21st Century Community Learning Centers Program is funded by the U.S. Department of Education to create or expand the role of community centers in providing academic enrichment activities to economically disadvantaged and other students in at-risk situations (TEA, 2005). One of the No Child Left Behind (NCLB) provisions requires that school districts make supplemental educational opportunities available to economically disadvantaged and other students in at-risk situations outside the regular school day (Flynn, 2002). In the 2003-2004 school year the typical 21st Century Community Learning Center program participant was economically disadvantaged, Hispanic, and enrolled in Kindergarten through Grade 5. Approximately one-third were classified as limited-English-proficient (LEP) and approximately 80 percent of the participants were classified as economically disadvantaged. It is important for Center and other tutoring personnel to know who the students are that they are serving. Often teachers and tutors are not prepared for the challenges presented by the students in after-school tutoring programs, especially those who are limited in their English proficiency. These students are often at risk of being left behind. Tutoring programs should be aimed at helping students achieve the success that they often miss in traditional classrooms.

According to Resnick (1991), it is important to understand that simply replicating the classroom environment in a different setting will more than likely produce negative results. It is necessary then to provide students with appropriate tutoring opportunities that will result in positive experiences. However, it is equally important and necessary when working with ELLs to use approaches that are designed with them in mind. Gallego, Rueda, and Moll (2003) contend that non-school settings are appealing because of their suitability for addressing diversity without the usual constraints of school. After-school programs that develop dual language opportunities for students also offer the possibility of more success with English Language Learners.

Hernández (2003) maintains that ELLs can enhance their learning skills more readily by learning study skills. Pérez and Torres-Guzman (1996) found that study skills could help ELLs identify general learning goals associated with academic success. These goals can be as simple as setting aside a specific routine time for quiet work and study. Hernández (2003) also believes that children's academic success depends directly on their ability to listen. The skill of listening is important since much of the classroom learning depends on good listening skills.

Research has demonstrated that schools that implement dual language approaches in working with English Language Learners have higher success rates than with other types of programmatic approaches (Lindholm-Leary, 2001; Calderón & Minaya-Rowe, 2003; Crawford, 2004). Dual language approaches, sometimes referred to as two-way bilingual "TWB" or two-way immersion "TWI," vary from community to community and at times from school to school. However, one of the highest performing programs is the 90-10 Model where approximately equal numbers of ELLs and native speakers of English are put into the same classes. These students typically begin their schooling experience by receiving 90% of their curriculum in the first language (for example Spanish), and 10% in English. The percentage of English is gradually increased so as to reach 50% by 5th and 6th grades (Lindholm-Leary, 2001).

There are other variations of this model such as the 50-50 Model and the Alicia Chacón Model in El Paso, Texas. As is implied by its title, the 50-50 Model integrates equal amounts of the two languages in its instructional delivery. The Alicia Chacón Model is described as a 'home-grown' model for teaching in three languages. It begins essentially as an 80-10-10 approach in kindergarten and eventually moves to a 45-45-10 program by 6th-8th grades. While the decision as to which approach will be used usually resides with school board members and administrators, both models have produced positive results and surpassed other forms of transitional bilingual education. Both models promoted proficiency in two languages although the 90-10 Model developed higher levels of bilingualism and higher levels of Spanish proficiency than the 50-50 Model (Calderón & Minaya-Rowe, 2003).

It would be reasonable then to expect that in-school tutoring programs as well as after-school programs that allow for the use of the native language in working with ELLs would also achieve a higher success rate. Bilingual education researchers have been able to establish that bilingual education programs work best at developing the academic use of both languages. Rolstad, Mahoney, and Glass (2005), state that bilingual education is superior to English-only approaches in increasing measures of students' academic achievement in English and in the native language. Although they point out that states such as California, Arizona, and Massachusetts have in recent years passed state laws by voter initiative, to either ban or severely discourage the use of native language instruction in their state school systems, teachers need to be knowledgeable of how to teach ELLs since their numbers are increasing despite the initiatives or bans. Also, research data by Cummins (1981), Ramírez (1992), and Collier (1987; 1992) suggest rather strongly that children in late-exit bilingual education programs seem to out-perform children in other types of programs, but especially English-only efforts. In light of the mounting evidence to support bilingual education, researchers conclude that teachers in bilingual education and ESL are needed now more than ever. For mainstream teachers, this means that the preparation for teaching ELLs is essential.

With the evidence in support of native language instruction for ELLs continues to be formidable, it is important to utilize this research in formulating in-school and after-school programs of the type aimed at improving achievement and closing the gap among ELLs. It is important to understand the student's language and cultural heritage in order to demonstrate a genuine interest in the student as well as allow the student to feel a sense of self-worth.

In summary, many factors affect the teaching of ELLs. These include the growing numbers of ELLs, the shortage of bilingual education and ESL teachers, the lack of preparation and professional development for preservice and inservice bilingual education, ESL, and mainstream teachers in linguistic, cultural, and content areas, promoting culturally responsive teachers, and the different types of programs available in dual language education. Since the typical participant in the 21st Century Community Learning Centers Program is economically disadvantaged, Hispanic, an English Language Learner, and enrolled at the K-5 level, the need to educate this large group of students is very apparent. The demographics of this group of students make it imperative that all of our teachers, schools, and community partners come together to ensure their success. In-school and after-school programs can serve to help close the existing achievement gap for these children.

Teachers and other school personnel working with ELLs must have knowledge of their students and language minority education in order to allow them to meet with success in the academic arena. Universities and particularly Colleges of Education must become more inclusive in order to attract more preservice teachers into the fields of bilingual and ESL education. Attracting a more diverse student body will allow these institutions of higher education to better prepare both preservice and inservice teachers who can serve as linguistic and cultural role models. This level of competence and understanding will help all teachers to meet the educational, language, and cultural needs of the ELLs in our schools. This will also assist in meeting the goal of producing more 'highly qualified' teachers. This type of academic preparation will ensure that teachers are prepared to meet the educational needs of all students—including those for whom English is not a first language.

As the numbers of ELLs continue to grow and as we become more aware of their educational needs, educators can no longer consciously practice "a culture of convenience." It is educationally and ethically wrong to expect ELLs to acquire a new language while not demonstrating value to the students' own heritage language, thus allowing them to lose it. Yet when they become adults, society will expect them to be fully bilingual. This cycle of being deficient in both languages must be broken. We must place students in 'win-win' educational situations by ensuring that their cultural, linguistic, and educational needs are addressed by all educators, allowing them to be successful in both the English and heritage language communities (Midobuche & Benavides, 2002-2003). We cannot continue to have ELLs sitting at the back of classrooms being ignored. Today's demographics should alert us to the immense need to change how we teach language minority children in order to avoid the mistakes of previous generations. Demographics should alert us to the immense need to change how we teach language minority children in order to avoid the mistakes of previous generations.

References

Abdelrahim. S. (2005, August). NCELA RAQ No. 24 Q: How can I become a teacher? OELA's National Clearinghouse for English Language Acquisition & Language Instruction Educational Programs. Retrieved March 9, 2006, from http://www.ncela.gwu.edu/expert/faq/24teacher.htm.

Abdelrahim. S. (2005, February). NCELA FAQ. 27 Q: How can I recruit teachers? OELA's National Clearinghouse for English Language Acquisition & Language Instruction Educational Programs. Retrieved March 9, 2006, from http://www.ncela.gwu.edu/expert/faq/27_teacher.html.

Associated Press. (2006, February). Dallas ISD proposes hiring illegal immigrants. OELA Newsline: Retrieved March 29, 2006, from http://www.ncela.gwu.edu/newsline/archives/2006/02/dallas_i sd_prop.html

Barbe, A. (January 21, 2006). JISD heads to Mexico to recruit bilingual teachers. Jacksonville Daily Progress (TX). Retrieved March 29, 2006, from http://www.jacksonvilleprogress.com/homepage/local_story_0 21155148.html?keyword=leadpicturestory

Boe, E. E. (1990). Demand, supply, and shortage of bilingual and ESL teachers: models, data, and policy issues. In *Proceedings of the first annual research symposium on Limited-English-proficient students' issues*. - Washington, D.C.: U.S. Department of Education, OBEMLA.

Calderón, M. E., & Minaya-Rowe, L. (2003). *Designing and implementing two-way bilingual programs*. Thousand Oaks, CA: Corwin Press, Inc.

Collier, V. P. (1987). Age and rate of acquisition of second language for academic purposes. *TESOL Quarterly, 21*, 617-641.

Collier, V. P. (1992). A synthesis of studies examining long-term language-minority student data on academic achievement. *Bilingual Research Journal, 16* (1, 2), 187-212.

Crawford, J. (2004). *Educating English Learners: Language diversity in the classroom*. Los Angeles: Bilingual Educational Services, Inc.

Crawford, J. (1997). *Best evidence: Research foundations of the Bilingual Education Act*. Retrieved March 9, 2006, from http://www.ncela.gwu.edu/pubs/reports/bestevidence/research. htm

Cummins, J. (2001). Assessment and intervention with culturally and linguistically diverse learners. In S. R. Hurley and J. V. Tinajero (Eds.), *Literacy assessment of second language learners* (pp. 115-129). Boston: Allyn and Bacon.

Cummins, J. (1981). The role of primary language development in promoting educational success for language minority students. In California State Department of Education (Ed.), *Schooling and language minority students: A theoretical framework* (pp. 3-49). Los Angeles: California State Department of Education.

Díaz, E. E. (2001). *Mexican immigrant children in urban Phoenix: Transitions to life, language, and school.* Unpublished doctoral dissertation, Arizona State University, Tempe.

Flynn, M. (2002) Title I supplemental educational services and after-school programs: Opportunities and challenges. New York: The Finance Report. Retrieved on December 15, 2005, from http://www.financeproject.org/publications/suppsvc.pdf

Gallego, M.A., Rueda, R., & Moll, L. C. (2003). Mediating language and literacy lessons from an after-school setting. In G.G. Garcia (Ed.), *English learners: Reaching the highest level of English literacy* (pp. 387-407). Newark, DE: Pearson.

Gándara, P. (1986). *Bilingual education: Learning English in California.* Sacramento: Assembly Office of Research.

Gold, N. C. (1992). Solving the shortage of bilingual teachers: Policy implications of California's staffing initiative for LEP students. *Proceedings of the third national research symposium on limited English proficient students issues.* Vol. 1, pp 223-278. Washington, DC: U.S. Department of Education, Office of Bilingual Education and Minority Languages Affairs.

Harvard Family Research Project. (August 2002). Beyond the head count: Evaluating family involvement in out of school time. Issues and opportunities in out of school time evaluation, 4. Retrieved on March 26, 2006, from http://www.gse.harvard.edu/hfrp/projects/afterschool/resource s/issuebrief4.html

Hernández, A. (2003) Making content instruction accessible for English language learners. In G.G. Garcia (Ed), *English learners: Reaching the highest level of English literacy* (pp. 125-149). Newark, DE: Pearson.

Lindhom-Leary K. J. (2001). *Dual language education.* Clevedon, England: Multilingual Matters.

Macias, R. F. (1989a). *Bilingual teacher supply and demand in the United States.* Los Angeles: University of California Center for Multilingual, Multicultural Research.

Menken, K., & Antunez, B. (2001). An overview of the preparation and certification of teachers working with limited English proficient students. NCELA. Retrieved on March 29, 2006, from http://www.ncela.gwu.edu/pubs/reports/teacherprep/teacherpre p.pdf

Menken, K., & Holmes, P. (2000). Ensuring English language learners' success: Balancing teacher quantity with quality. NCBE. Retrieved March 9, 2006, from http://www.ncela.gwu.edu/pubs/tasynthesis/framing/5teacherq uality.htm

Midobuche, E., & Benavides, A.H. (2002-2003). Language attitudes and the culture of convenience: Placing students in a no-win situation. *National Forum of Applied Educational Research Journal, 15*(4), 73-80.

Midobuche, E. (2001a). More than empty footprints in the sand: Educating immigrant children. *Harvard Educational Review 27*(3), 529-535.

Midobuche, E. (2001b). Bridging the culture gap between home and school through mathematics. *Teaching Children Mathematics* 7(9), 500-502.

Midobuche, E. (1999). Respect in the classroom: Reflections of a Mexican American educator. *Educational Leadership 56* (7), 80-82.

Midobuche, E., Benavides, A. H., Angulo, T., Canales, L., Flores, C., Hernandez, J., & Lopez, J. (2006, March). *Closing the gap for English language learners: Expanding academic opportunities through 21st century community learning centers.* Symposium conducted at the National Association for Multicultural Education (NAME) Conference, Lubbock, Texas.

Midobuche, E., Benavides, A. H., & Diaz, E. (2006, January). *4 Cs + 4 Rs = Catalysts for educating Mexican immigrant students.* Paper presented at the annual meeting of the National Association for Bilingual Education (NABE), Phoenix, Arizona.

Moss, M., & Puma, M. (1995). *Prospects: The congressionally mandated study of educational growth and opportunity. First year report on language minority and limited-English-proficient students.* Cambridge, MA: Abt Associates.

Murdock, S. H. (2002). *A summary of the Texas challenge in the twenty-first century: Implications of population changes for the future of Texas.* Center for Demographic and Socio-economic Research and Education, Department of Rural Sociology, Texas A&M University. Retrieved on February 1, 2006, from http://txsdc.utsa.edu/pubsrep/pubs/txchal.php.

National Association of Elementary School Principals (1993). *Standards for quality school-age child care.* Alexandria, VA: National Association of Elementary School Principals.

National Institute on Out-of-School Time. (2003). *Make the case: A fact sheet on children and youth in out of school time.* Center for Research on Women, College. Retrieved on March

23, 2006, from
http://www.niost.org/publications/Factsheet_2003.PDF.
National Clearinghouse for English Language Acquisition &
Language Instruction Educational Programs. (2004). *The
growing numbers of LEP students, 2001-2004.* Office of
English Language Acquisition, Department of Education.
Retrieved October 3, 2005, from
http://www.ncela.gwu.edu/stats/2_nation.htm
NCELA (2002). Languages, 2000-2001 ranked by number of
speakers. Office of English Language Acquisition. Retrieved
March 28, 2006, from
http://www.ncela.gwu.edu/stats/4_toplanguages/languages.ht
ml.
Perez, B., & Torres-Guzman, M. (1996). *Learning in two worlds.*
White Plains, NY: Longman.
Quezada, M. (1991). *District remedies to eliminate the shortage of
qualified teachers of limited English proficient students in
California.* Unpublished doctoral dissertation, University of
Southern California.
Ramírez, J. D. (1992). Executive summary. *Bilingual Research
Journal 16,* 1-62.
Resnick, L. (1991). Literacy in and out of school. In S.R.
Graubard (Ed.), *Literacy: An overview of fourteen experts*
(pp.169-185). New York: Noonday Press.
Rolstad, K., Mahoney, K., & Glass, G. (2005, September). The
big picture: A meta-analysis of program effectiveness
research on English language learners. *Educational Policy 19*
(4), 592-594.
TESOL. (2003). *TESOL/NCATE standards for P-12 teacher
education programs.* Retrieved December 3, 2005, from
http://www.tesol.org/s_tesol/seccss.asp?CID=219&DID=1689
Texas Education Agency (January, 2005). *21st century community
learning centers: Evaluation of project funded for the 2003-04
school year.* Austin, TX: Author.

Texas Education Agency (2005) *Division of performance reporting, academic excellence indicator system (AEIS) 2004-2005 state performance report.* Retrieved February 2, 2006, from http://www.tea.state.tx.us/perfreport/aeis/2005/state.html.

Torres-Guzman, M. E., & Goodwin, A. L. (1995). Mentoring bilingual teachers. *NCBE FOCUS: Occasional Papers in Bilingual Education*, Number 12, Fall 1995. Retrieved March 19, 2006, from http://www.ncela.gwu.edu/pubs/focus/focus12.htm

U.S. Department of Education. (2003). *21st century community learning centers non-regulatory guidance.* Washington, DC: Author. Retrieved March 26, 2006, from http://www.ed.gov/programs/21stcclc/guidance2003.pdf.

U. S. Department of Education. (2002). *21st Century community learning centers program honored with public service award.* Washington, DC: Author. Retrieved March 17, 2006, from http://www.ed.gov/news/pressreleases/2002/06/06182002.html.

U.S. Department of Education, National Center for Education Statistics (2002*). Schools and staffing survey, 1999-2000: Overview of the data for public, private, public charter, and bureau of Indian Affairs elementary and secondary schools.* Washington, DC: Author. Table 1.19. pp. 43-44. Retrieved March 29, 2006, from http://nces.ed.gov/pubsearch/pubsinfo.asp?pubid=2002313 and from http://nces.ed.gov/pubs2002/2002313.pdf.

Villegas, A.M., & Lucas, T. (2002). Preparing culturally responsive teachers: Rethinking the curriculum. *Journal of Teacher Education*, 53, (1), 20-32.

Meeting the Needs of Newcomer non-Spanish Speaking ELLs:
A Case Study of Two Cambodian Students in a Suburban Intermediate School

Wayne E. Wright
University of Texas at San Antonio

Mrs. Moore had just moved to the San Antonio, TX area from Maine and signed up as a substitute in a nearby school district. She had taught for a few years in other states where she had lived, but had never worked with English language learners (ELLs), and did not have any kind of English as a second language (ESL) training. One day in mid-September she was substituting at Rodgers Intermediate School, and by the end of the day, was hired to take over a 5th grade class for a teacher who was leaving. One month later, she was eating lunch with the school's attendance clerk, who smiled at her and asked, "Has the principal talked to you yet?" "No, why?" Mrs. Moore asked. "There are two little girls from Cambodia that came in to register today, and they are trying to figure out where to put them. They don't speak any English." Friday afternoon, Mrs. Moore asked her principal about the girls. The principal replied, "Oh, yes, we've decided to put them in your class. They start on Monday!" On Monday morning the principal brought two nervous-looking rail-thin girls, Nitha and Bora, into Mrs. Moore's classroom. "Here they are!" the principal exclaimed. "Is there anything you need?" "Well," Mrs.

Moore said, feeling a bit overwhelmed, "for starters, I'll need two more desks."

Situations similar to the one above regularly occur in schools throughout Texas and the United States (National Clearinghouse for English Language Acquisition, 2003). An increasing number of teachers are finding themselves face-to-face with newly-arrived ELL students in their classrooms, whom they feel ill-prepared to teach (Ariza, 2006; Crawford, 2004). While many schools in Texas offer bilingual education programs which are well suited to newly-arrived Spanish-speaking ELLs (Perez, 2003; Program Evaluation Unit, 2000), few Texas schools offer bilingual programs in any other language. Indeed, while Spanish-speakers make up 94% of the over 520,000 ELL students in Texas, there are over 37,000 ELLs in the state who speak a wide variety of other languages, including Cantonese, Mandarin, Russian, Vietnamese, Urdu, Korean, Arabic, Khmer, Lao, and their numbers are increasing each year.

Non-Spanish-speaking ELLs are often placed in English-only mainstream classrooms, and, unfortunately, many are simply left there to "sink-or-swim" with little to no services or support (Baker, 2001; Baker & Jones, 1998; Wright, 2004). This study, however, documents the efforts of the faculty and staff of Rodgers Intermediate School to meet the language and academic needs of its two newly-arrived Cambodian students. Despite several problems and frustrations, this school's response nonetheless demonstrates how a school and individual teachers can assist and support newly-arrived ELL students, using available resources. This school's experience is instructive for other schools and their teachers who are facing similar challenges in meeting the needs of newly-arrived ELLs, particularly those for whom no bilingual education programs are available.

In this paper, I provide a brief overview of Rodgers Intermediate School, followed by an introduction to Nitha and Bora, the newly arrived Cambodian students. Next I will describe the school's rationale for placing Nitha and Bora in Mrs. Moore's classroom, and then describe the various strategies and techniques used by her to try to meet their needs. A description of a number of other support services provided outside of Mrs. Moore's classroom, including pull-out ESL instruction, assistance from a paraprofessional, computer lab instruction, and primary language support will follow. The paper concludes with a description of the progress made by Nitha and Bora by the end of the school year. Implications and lessons other schools and teachers may learn from this school's experience will be provided.

Methodology

This qualitative research case study utilized participant observation, interviews with teachers and support personnel, and the collection and analysis of school-based documents (e.g., policy documents, memos, notes, lesson plans, curricular materials, student work, progress reports, assessments, etc.). Soon after the arrival of Nitha and Bora, I began volunteering at the school to provide Khmer primary language support during one-hour tutoring sessions each week, which continued until the end of the school year (see below for details). In addition, I conducted observations in their regular and ESL classrooms and in their tutoring sessions with the paraprofessional and in the computer lab. Digital audio recordings were made and field notes were taken during my tutoring session and observations described above. Formal interviews were conducted with the classroom teacher, ESL teacher, and the paraprofessional. These interviews were digitally audio-recorded and fully transcribed. Detailed field notes were also kept on informal conversations with these individuals and others, including the school counselor, principal, the computer lab teacher, other teachers and paraprofessionals, and the girls themselves. Fieldnotes, transcripts, and documents were imported into and organized using *QSR Nvivo*, a qualitative data analysis software program. Data analysis was guided by the work of Erickson (1986) and Miles and Huberman (1994). To maintain confidentiality, the names of the students, teachers and staff, and school are pseudonyms.

Rodgers Intermediate School

Rodgers Intermediate School is in a medium-sized school district of 13 schools serving 7,636 students in grades PreK-12. The district is located in a suburb on the outskirts of San Antonio in a rapidly growing area. Rodgers provides instruction to 590 students in grades 5 and 6. Over half of the students are White (58%), while 29% are Hispanic and 10% are African American, and only 2% are Asian/Pacific Islanders. The school is located in a middle-class neighborhood, and only 31% participate in the free/reduced lunch program (well below the state average of 53%). English language learners represent less than 1% of the schools' enrollment. In the 2004-2005 school year, Rodgers was rated as "academically acceptable" by the Texas Education Agency (District and School information retrieved from www.greatschools.net).

Nitha and Bora

Nitha and Bora are sisters who arrived with their father (and one other sister) in the middle of October 2004. In Cambodia, they lived in a poor village in Takeo Province, far from their provincial capital or any major cities. Their family was sponsored to the United States by relatives who run a small but successful business (donut shop). They live with their relatives in a spacious two-story home—a far cry from the one-room thatched hut with no electricity or running water where they used to live. While no school records were provided at the time of enrollment, it was later determined that both girls had attended school in their village; Nitha had completed 6th grade, and Bora had completed the 4th grade. Despite the poor condition of Cambodian schools (Ministry of Education, 2004; Planning Department, 2006; Um, 1999), particularly in the rural areas, both girls had strong Khmer (Cambodian) literacy skills, and could do basic arithmetic. While both were reportedly excellent students, neither had studied English before coming to the United States, nor could they speak a single word of English upon their arrival. Both Nitha and Bora faced the challenges of living and attending school in a new country with a strange language, customs, and food.

Placement Decision

Traditionally students in 5th grade at Rodgers were placed in "clusters" and rotated between the four 5th grade teachers, each of whom taught a different subject. However, at the beginning of the 2004-2005 school year, rapid growth in the student population necessitated the addition of a new 5th grade classroom, and rather than disrupt the four-teacher cluster rotation system, it was decided that this new classroom would be "self-contained" (i.e., one teacher teaches all subjects). School administrators also decided before the beginning of the school year to put all three of the school's 5th grade ELL students in the self-contained classroom, under the rationale that the teacher assigned to the class was bilingual in English and Spanish. However, this teacher did not have any bilingual or ESL certification or training, and the three ELLs assigned to her did not speak Spanish (they spoke Thai, Tagalog, and Swedish). The teacher was promoted after the first month of school to an administrative position at another school. As described in the vignette at the beginning of this article, Mrs. Moore was hired after one day of substituting at the school to take over the self-contained 5th grade classroom.

When Nitha and Bora arrived one month later, the administrators struggled with where to place them. They decided to keep the girls together in the same classroom and grade level, despite their age differences, so that they would feel less frightened and could provide support to each other in the classroom. It was further decided to place them in the self-contained classroom, as this would be less confusing (i.e., they would not have to switch classrooms every hour). In addition it was where the other ELL students were placed, and thus would make it easier for the ESL teacher to pull them out. These decisions were made despite the fact that one of the rotation teachers had received some ESL training the previous summer, and that Mrs. Moore had none. Despite Mrs. Moore's lack of training and experience with ELL students, she worked hard to meet their needs in the classroom, and was a strong advocate for getting them help and support outside of the classroom, as will be discussed in the following sections.

Classroom instruction

Mrs. Moore had 25 students in her classroom when Nitha and Bora arrived. The three ELL students already in her classroom were at the intermediate and advanced levels of English language proficiency, and able to do most of the regular work in the class. Mrs. Moore described the first few days in her classroom with Nitha and Bora as "extremely challenging." The school's ESL teacher, Mrs. Leonard, was out that week attending meetings, and thus was not able to offer support. Mrs. Moore remembers, "The first day, I was in tears by lunch." The girls just sat at the back table and couldn't understand a word of what she was saying, nor could she understand them. Lunchtime, however, proved to be the first major challenge. Mrs. Moore struggled to help the girls pick out food in the cafeteria they could eat, and ended up arguing with the cafeteria manager over mandatory food choices and payment of the meal. The girls' application for free-reduced lunch had not yet been processed, so Mrs. Moore paid for them out of her own pocket. Other simple things proved to be major challenges as well, such as just trying to help them get their backpacks at the end of day. Mrs. Moore recalled, "The first day was extremely overwhelming."

When Nitha and Bora first arrived, the principal suggested, "They will just want to be immersed in the classroom in English, so, they'll just sit there." But Mrs. Moore determined that simply letting them "just sit there" would not be acceptable:

> They seemed almost frustrated because you can imagine, six hours of just sitting and listening and not knowing what anyone is saying, was not working. I didn't know what was going to happen the second day, but then I just decided, "you know what, I am going to start with colors." I had to get them started on something.

She found some very simple worksheets on colors the girls could do fairly independently. She admitted it was basically to keep them busy with something to do, but, as she said, "it was a start." Bora did not complain, but Mrs. Moore remembers that Nitha seemed a little insulted with this "baby work."

When Mrs. Leonard returned the following week, she was only able to work with Nitha and Bora for 30 minutes, three times a week. She knew they needed more assistance, but could not offer them more time because she was also covering two other schools. After a few weeks, Mrs. Moore continued to feel overwhelmed. She recalls:

> I felt bad for them. I didn't have a lot of experience, and we don't have any resources in here for that level. And when I asked about resources, "Could I go to the elementary school to the ESL teachers and pull some of their stuff?"

and I was told "No," and that I needed to differentiate fifth-grade curriculum material. I said, "Great! Come show me how."

Despite her requests for assistance, no one came to show her what to do or how to help Nitha and Bora learn the regular 5th grade curriculum. Mrs. Moore realized she was on her own. A major focus of the regular instruction, she noted with regret, was to prepare students for the Texas Assessment of Knowledge and Skills (TAKS), and she was required to use a language arts program and a math curricular program that were specifically designed for that purpose. She determined that such instruction and materials were inappropriate and inaccessible for her two newcomers. Instead, she decided to differentiate her instruction by providing separate lessons and activities that were more appropriate to Nitha and Bora's level of English and academic skills.

Mrs. Moore bought several educational games that her other students could play with Nitha and Bora. She searched her garage at home and found many materials from the year she taught Kindergarten, including several books with audiotapes the girls could listen to and follow along with at the listening center. During the first week, she had students take them around the school to meet the administrators, staff, and specialists they would see each week. They took pictures of each person they met, then used the photos to create a book. Mrs. Moore had other students read to them and do simple activities with them in class. She created a classroom atmosphere where the other students were welcoming and anxious to help Nitha and Bora. Mrs. Moore noted that some took to "mothering" them.

In terms of academic instruction, Mrs. Moore prepared lessons and activities each day that were similar to what she was teaching the rest of the students, but at a more appropriate level. She obtained relevant worksheets and materials that were more at a 1st or 2nd grade level. For example, when she was working with her students on Math doing complex (TAKS-like) multi-step word problems, she had Nitha and Bora working on simple computational worksheets, and simple one-step word problems. In a social studies unit in which students were expected to learn the capital and basic facts about each state, Mrs. Moore worked with Nitha and Bora to help them understand what a state is, and to learn the names of each state. In science, while the rest of the students engaged in an in-depth lesson on the rock cycle, she worked with Nitha and Bora to understand what a "cycle" is, and had them do simple art-type projects on the water cycle and the life cycle of a butterfly. For language arts, as the other students worked on TAKS-preparatory reading comprehension exercises, Nitha and Bora worked on basic reading skills, and played sight word games and other activities to learn new vocabulary.

Mrs. Moore created a different set of 10 spelling words primarily consisting of sight words for Nitha and Bora each week. She attempted to explain the meaning of each word through pictures or by having them look up the words in their bilingual Khmer-English dictionary (see below), and would have them draw a picture next to each word to illustrate its meaning. She had an established in-class and homework routine for them to practice writing and spelling their words each week. Nitha and Bora studied hard and both would typically earn 100% on their spelling tests each week.

Still, Mrs. Moore was frustrated. She recognized that the Nitha and Bora needed more support than she was able to give them on her own. She found it increasingly difficult to work with them one-on-one each day. Whenever she attempted to do so, a long line of her other students needing help with their independent seatwork would form behind her. An aide assigned to the classroom part of the day began to work with Nitha and Bora, but she was frequently pulled out by the office to cover for other teachers or staff members. Mrs. Moore was discouraged as many of the lessons and activities she had prepared for the aide to do with Nitha and Bora would fall by the wayside.

After a few months, Mrs. Moore was so discouraged and overwhelmed that she called for a meeting with the administrators and other staff members. Together, they came up with a more comprehensive plan to meet Nitha and Bora's language and academic needs. Some of the components of this plan are outlined below.

Pull-out ESL

The school's ESL teacher, Mrs. Leonard, while relatively new to Rodgers Intermediate School, had over 27 years of ESL teaching experience. Prior to Nitha and Bora's arrival, Mrs. Leonard had only been working with five ELL students in the school, in addition to monitoring a handful of others who had exited from the program. Her time at the school was limited as she was also servicing two other schools in the district. As mentioned above, she initially only had 30 minutes, three times a week to work with Nitha and Bora, which she lamented was not nearly enough. She had joked at one point with Mrs. Moore, calling herself the "drive-by ESL teacher." She also did her best to provide materials for Mrs. Moore and offer her suggestions, but her schedule did not allow her to spend much time offering support.

Mrs. Leonard raised the issue with the district, reporting that her students at Rodgers needed more support than she was able to give. Finally, in February 2005, the district hired a full-time ESL teacher for one of the other school sites, thus allowing Mrs. Leonard to spend more time at Rodgers. From that point on, she was able to work with Nitha and Bora daily for one hour and fifteen minutes in the afternoon.

When Mrs. Leonard first came into the school, she found that the district had not adopted any specific ESL curricular programs or purchased many ESL supplemental materials for the 5th grade. Those materials that the school did have were, as she described them, "antiquated." She used the small budget she had to purchase materials, and bought many more out of her own pocket. She also described her efforts to "beg and borrow" as many materials as she could from textbook company representatives and other teachers. Through these efforts she assembled an eclectic set of resources she could pull from as she tailored her instruction to the needs of each individual student.

The ESL classroom was in a bungalow which was colorfully decorated with a variety of charts and other visuals useful for teaching basic vocabulary, e.g., calendar, days of the week, months of the year, and shapes. Around the classroom on chalkboard ledges were displays of a large number of simple books, all related to a specific theme. This print-rich environment Mrs. Leonard created in her classroom was conducive to the language and literacy development for ELL students (Hadaway, Vardell, and Young, 2002).

Nitha and Bora worked with Mrs. Leonard in a small group with one other girl from their class, an intermediate level ELL from Thailand. Mrs. Leonard described what it was like when she first started working with Nitha and Bora:

> It was kind of slow going in the beginning. But I've known from my experiences in the past that that is to be expected and I needed to respect that. I just wanted to, first of all, make them feel comfortable and feel where they could be in an environment that was non-threatening. We know about that affective filter and how kids will shut down if they're not feeling comfortable about taking opportunities and risks to acquire any language or any learning.

Observations conducted in Mrs. Leonard's ESL classroom verified that she succeeded in creating the type of warm, non-threatening environment, which, as she herself noted, is important to lower the affective filter of students so that comprehensible input can be maximized (Krashen, 1985, 2003). It was apparent that Nitha and Bora were very comfortable in their ESL classroom. While they were typically quiet in their regular classroom, in here they were active, engaged, and unafraid to take risks in using their new language. Their ESL classroom created opportunities for the type of meaningful listening and speaking interactions which are necessary for ELLs to acquire English (Haley & Austin, 2003).

The students engaged in a wide variety of activities in the ESL classroom. Mrs. Leonard established a number of routines surrounding the calendar and the various charts around the room and utilized them to teach basic vocabulary. Each session, students would pull out a slip of paper from a hat Mrs. Leopold would pass around, which indicated the routine they would be responsible for leading. These routines were fun and more game-like than repetitious drills or worksheet, and thus proved effective in helping the students learn new vocabulary (Nation, 2001).

Mrs. Leonard utilized thematic teaching and engaged students in meaningful hands-on interactive activities surrounding these themes (Freeman & Freeman, 1998). For example, for the theme "The five senses," Mrs. Leonard brought in many items from home for students to see, hear, smell, touch, and taste. In one activity, students reached into a mystery box and used their sense of touch to guess what item was in the box. She read aloud simple books related to the five senses. Students made posters for each of the five senses by cutting pictures out of magazines. Students wrote in their journal completing sentences written on the board such as "I can _____ with my eyes" and "I can listen with my _____." During the theme of "plants," in addition to similar activities as those above, Mrs. Leonard engaged the students in hands-on experiments with growing plants from various types of seeds. These thematic lessons and others integrated listening, speaking, reading and writing in effective ways which helped these ELL students develop communicative competence in their new language (Lee & Van Patten, 2003).

As Nitha, Bora, and their classmate engaged in these activities, Mrs. Leonard did not simply let them work independently as she sat at her desk. Rather, she worked with them throughout, talking with them the entire time. She used the activities to model the key vocabulary and language needed to talk about the tasks they were completing, and to engage the students in meaningful conversations to use their new vocabulary to accomplish the tasks she had given them. These strategies increased the students' opportunities for "incidental learning" of vocabulary, that is, learning vocabulary subconsciously by using language for communicative purposes (Schmitt, 2000). Mrs. Leonard adjusted her speech to a slower but appropriate pace for beginning ELLs, and she carefully controlled the vocabulary and structure of her sentences (Echevarria, Vogt, & Short, 2004). She utilized repetition, gestures, visuals, and other techniques to make her speech understandable, thus increasing her students' comprehensible input (Krashen, 1985).

She also had the students engaged in a number of literacy activities, especially reading books appropriately matched to their language and reading level (Hadaway, Vardell, & Young, 2002). Mrs. Leonard had a number of guided-reading type books designed for emergent readers (Pinnell & Fountas, 1996), which contain simple repetitive sentences with ample visual support in the illustrations or photographs (Peregoy & Boyle, 2000). For example, one book entitled *Do You Like My Pet?* (Tripp, 1999) had one simple sentence per page such as "Do you like my dog?" and "Do you like my duck?" with each being accompanied by a photograph of a child holding their respective pet animal. By using these books to teach vocabulary, and through repeated readings, soon Nitha and Bora had a large collection of books that they could read with confidence and pride.

Nitha and Bora clearly benefited from their time with Mrs. Leonard in the ESL pull-out classroom. They were at ease in a supportive environment, and Mrs. Leonard used her expertise to create a variety of meaningful, engaging, and fun activities to support their English language acquisition (Beykont, 2002; Echevarria, 2002; Freeman & Freeman, 1998; Peregoy & Boyle, 2004). Given the small size of the group, Mrs. Leonard was able to give each student the kind of individual attention and tailored instruction that Mrs. Moore found was difficult to provide in her large regular classroom. As the months progressed, the amount of English the girls learned and used with their teacher, their classmates, and even with each other, increased dramatically.

Paraprofessional assistance

A major part of Mrs. Moore's frustration was not being able to spend enough classroom time with Nitha and Bora. Especially at the beginning, there was little that they could do independently. They needed someone to work with them the whole time to guide them through a worksheet or activity. Following her plea for help in the meeting with the administrators, they arranged for Mrs. Davis, a paraprofessional who had been assigned to the school counselor, to work with Nitha and Bora for an hour or more each morning. Mrs. Davis had been working at the school as a teacher's aide for over ten years, and at one point had also worked briefly as a substitute teacher. However, she did not hold teacher certification, nor had she previously worked with ELL students or received any type of ESL training. Nonetheless, she is a friendly and outgoing person, and was more than happy to work with Nitha and Bora. Reflecting back on what it was like when she first started working with them, Mrs. Davis described it as a real challenge given her lack of experience. She remembers trying to talk with them, but only getting blank stares in return: "They were looking at me, like, what are you talking about? No clue!" In just a short time, however, Mrs. Davis found working with Nitha and Bora a "real joy." She described how she looked forward to working with them everyday, "It really gives me a good feeling because it feels like I can accomplish something with the girls, and they are so eager to learn." From observations of her sessions, it was readily apparent the Nitha and Bora adored Mrs. Davis as well.

Mrs. Davis' assistance made it possible for Mrs. Moore to plan more in-depth lessons and activities for Nitha and Bora. Mrs. Moore spent time each week planning lessons and gathering materials which were similar to what she was doing with her other students, but at a more appropriate language and academic level. Each day she would give Mrs. Davis the materials and instructions, and Mrs. Davis would do her best to help the girls understand what to do. She also began to supplement the lessons herself, and even started to do extra activities with them, such as teaching Nitha and Bora about Halloween, Thanksgiving, Christmas and other holidays. But mostly, she just talked with the girls. Unlike Mrs. Leonard, she did not appear to adjust her rate of speech or even attempt to carefully control her vocabulary. She just talked. Nevertheless, despite Nitha and Bora's limited vocabulary, after a couple of months, Mrs. Davis and the girls were genuinely communicating, albeit on a very basic level. They appeared to be able to understand each other and were clearly enjoying their conversations.

Reflecting back on Mrs. Davis' work, Mrs. Moore acknowledged that the academic work often took a back seat, but said she viewed their time with Mrs. Davis as "oral language heaven." Indeed it was. Like their time with Mrs. Leonard, Nitha and Bora had another set time during the day with a caring adult who simply took the time to talk with them, and thus created a risk-free environment to practice listening and speaking in their new language, usually (but not always) surrounding an academic task. While she may not have been aware of or known the technical terms, Mrs. Davis was successful in lowering Nitha and Bora's affective filter, and provided ample comprehensible input, which leads to greater English language acquisition (Krashen, 2003).

Computer lab

Another support for Nitha and Bora came through the school's computer lab. The lab, run by a paraprofessional, Mrs. Stone, had a number of older PC computers, and utilized a somewhat outdated software program by Compass Learning (see www.compasslearning.com for similar but more current programs). The software program contained self-guided lessons for reading and math, and were designed to start students at their appropriate reading and math levels and then help them progress to higher levels from there. The program kept track of their progress, and students could not move to the next lesson or level until they demonstrated sufficient progress by answering all questions within the current lesson correctly.

While this software program was not designed for ELL students, it nonetheless contained several features that proved to be supportive for Nitha and Bora. The program contained engaging and lively graphics. Students could wear headphone and hear all instructions and other texts read aloud to them. If they read on their own, they could click on any word they did not know and hear it read aloud. If they continued to answer questions or do activities wrong, the computer would model the correct answer. The types of questions and activities were similar across the lessons; thus, once students completed a few lessons, they felt familiar and comfortable with the program. In addition, Mrs. Davis would frequently come into the lab with the girls to provide them with assistance, and Mrs. Stone also monitored their progress and provided help when needed.

Despite the fact that they were in a 5th grade classroom, all students were able to work simultaneously at their own level. Nitha and Bora started the Reading and Math programs at the Kindergarten level, and by early May they had both completed the K and 1st grade levels and began to work on Grade 2. Thus, over a seven-month period, both Nitha and Bora made over two years' progress in these important content areas.

Primary language support

One other significant support the school provided Nitha and Bora was assistance in their primary language (Jesness, 2004; Wright, in-press). Ovando, Combs and Collier (2006), assert that "the research evidence is very clear that first-language development provides crucial support for second language development," and note the importance of allowing beginning ESL students to use their first language (p. 154). As noted by Wright (in press), there are ways teachers can provide primary language support, even when they do not speak their students' languages.

Some of these strategies were utilized by the teachers and staff at Rodgers.

Mrs. Leopold, Mrs. Moore, and Mrs. Davis all allowed Nitha and Bora to speak to each other in Khmer.[1] Not only did this provide moral support, but it also enabled them to work together to comprehend academic tasks. When one of the girls understood a direction or a task, she would explain it to the other in Khmer. Nitha and Bora were also excited to receive two copies of a Khmer-English Picture Dictionary (Shapiro & Adelson-Goldstein, 1999) that Mrs. Leopold was able to obtain from a textbook representative she knew, who was willing to donate the dictionaries to the school. The girls were able to use the dictionaries in their classroom, and their teachers and others were also able to use them on occasion to point to pictures, words, and their Khmer translations when they had difficulty getting certain ideas across (Summers, 1988). Later, other relevant Khmer language materials were obtained covering social studies and math concepts taught in class. In one observation, Nitha made the connection between a social studies lesson Mrs. Moore was teaching and an entry in the Khmer social studies book she had been given. She quickly pulled out the book and turned to the appropriate section. The Khmer social studies text provided her with important background knowledge which helped her understand better the lesson being taught in class (Echevarria, Vogt, & Short, 2004). Teachers also encouraged Nitha and Bora to write notes in Khmer. Mrs. Moore even had them make a few posters in class, such as the days of the week, in which they were able to write in both English and Khmer. They would also sometimes write Khmer translations next to their spelling words.

However, Mrs. Moore, especially at the beginning, felt completely overwhelmed and frustrated as she and others had great difficulty even communicating with the girls. A colleague across the hall sympathetic to her plight suggested that they find a community volunteer who could speak Khmer. She suggested that with the large military presence in San Antonio, there had to be someone who could speak the language. She called one of the Air Force bases which had a school mentoring program. Unable to find someone who could speak Khmer, e-mails were sent out to different agencies and organizations in the community. One of the e-mails eventually made it to the University of Texas, San Antonio, where I had joined the faculty just two months prior.

When I received an e-mail about the school's need, I was both surprised and excited. San Antonio had a very small Cambodian population and I had assumed my Khmer language skills would be of little use here. The Air Force mentoring program put me in contact with the school's counselor, and a few weeks later I began volunteering at the school for an hour or more a week to provide Khmer primary language support. Mrs. Moore told me later that she was so pleased to learn that someone was coming to assist with native language support.

One of my first tasks was to get answers to a long list of questions Mrs. Moore and others had regarding the students' background, particularly in terms of their prior schooling and to what level they could read and write and do math in their own language. I talked to Nitha and Bora about their schooling in Cambodia and they described to me what they had learned in school prior to moving to the United States. Both proudly noted that they were top students in their class. After conducting a few informal assessments, I determined that they had strong Khmer literacy skills, and that their math and computational skills were excellent by Cambodian grade-level standards, but far from what is expected of students in the same grade level in Texas. There were also a number of basic safety issues such as "Don't run out into the street." and "Use the cross walk." that the school was anxious for me to help them understand.

Once these issues were resolved, Mrs. Moore began planning lessons and selecting appropriate materials for me to work on with Nitha and Bora each week. She decided to have our Khmer primary language tutoring sessions focus primarily on math. As dictated by the federal No Child Left Behind policy, Nitha and Bora were exempt as newcomer ELLs from taking the Language Arts segment of the Texas Assessment of Knowledge and Skills (TAKS), but were nonetheless required to take the Math TAKS test in the Spring (Wiley & Wright, 2004; Wright, 2005). While Mrs. Moore had little expectation that Nitha and Bora would be able to pass the TAKS test after only a few months of schooling in the United States, she felt math would be an important area on which to focus. Mrs. Moore explained during the interview that she would save the "hard" stuff for me, meaning those mathematical concepts and procedures that she and Mrs. Davis were having difficulty explaining to Nitha and Bora in English. Mrs. Leonard also made a few requests on occasion of content she wanted to make sure the girls understood. On occasion there would also be work from social studies and science, and sometimes my services were needed by the teachers, counselor or nurse to help resolve small crises and misunderstandings, but the majority of the Khmer primary language support time focused on math instruction.

I found, as had the others above, that Nitha and Bora were intelligent, determined, hard working, and a joy to work with. Our initial sessions began with two- and three-digit addition and subtraction (with regrouping). As the school year progressed, we worked on fractions, decimals, money, probability, and solving one-step and later two-step word problems. I was impressed at how quickly they grasped new concepts once they were explained to them in their native language.

At the end of year, both Mrs. Moore and Mrs. Leonard commented on how effective they felt the primary language support had been. Mrs. Moore described it as "extremely helpful," and commented:

> First of all, it was helpful for me to see them light up when they know you are coming. They love it. And you can imagine, I mean, the one day a week they get to hear their language and they get to understand what's going on that whole afternoon period. ... And I can clearly see in the [math] story problems ... they're circling those key words, doing the best that they can.

Mrs. Leonard described the primary language support as "a tremendous help to Nitha and Bora," and commented:

> I can't say enough about all that you've done for the girls, ... taking time to visit with them, clarifying things, giving them some additional instruction. You have made the process so much better, not only for the kids, but [also] for us as their teachers.

Nitha, however, made the most telling comment. During one tutoring session we were working on fractions, which Mrs. Moore reported Nitha and Bora had been struggling with all week. After a very brief explanation, Nitha and Bora both let out an excited "Oh!" indicating they finally understood the concept. They both began to rapidly complete their fractions worksheets. About halfway through, Nitha said to me, "When you explain it in Khmer, it's so easy."

Nitha and Bora's progress

Nitha and Bora began the school year over two months after the beginning of the school year, and entered the 5th grade not knowing a single word in English. They did not pass the Math TAKS test, nor did they become proficient in English after seven months of instruction. However, the progress they made both in learning English and academic content was impressive. At an end-of-the-year party in Mrs. Leonard's ESL classroom, Nitha and Bora, along with the other ELL students, played host to their teachers, administrators and other school guests. They each had a basket full of books they eagerly and proudly read one-on-one with their guests. In their classroom and other areas of the school, they were able to hold basic conversations with their teachers and new friends. Bora even got in trouble on occasion for passing notes— written in English—to her friends in class. Both consistently earned high marks on their weekly spelling tests and other quizzes.

Mrs. Moore also noted significant improvement in Nitha and Bora's math knowledge and skills. During the first month, she started them with math instruction at the kindergarten level. Seven months later, she described Nitha as at-grade level in terms of computation, and at the 3rd to 4th grade level in terms of solving problems requiring greater use of language. Bora, who is younger, also made significant progress. Mrs. Moore reported that Bora was reading at about the 1st grade level, while Nitha was at about the 2nd grade level. Mrs. Moore described Nitha as "quite the reader," and found that she could decode at a much higher level than she could comprehend. But by the end of the year, Nitha was stating to read *Cam Jansen* chapter books (Adler & Natti, 2002), a popular series among students of her age.

Conclusion and implications

When two non-English-speaking Cambodian students enrolled at Rodgers Intermediate School, it would have been very easy for their teacher to simply let them sit in the back of a mainstream classroom to "sink-or-swim" (Baker & Jones, 1998). Unfortunately, this happens often at schools throughout the state and country, especially for many non-Spanish-speaking newly-arrived ELL students for whom bilingual programs may not be available. Corson (2001) makes a strong case for bilingual education, arguing that students should have the right to learn standard English *and* be educated in the "language that is learned at home." However, he acknowledges that it may not be practicable for schools to offer a bilingual program, particularly in schools like Rodgers where there are several different languages and only one or two speakers of each language. In these cases, Corson argues there are two principles that should be met: (a) students should have the right to "attend a school that shows full respect for the language variety that is learned at home or valued most by them," and (b) students should have the right "to learn, to the highest level of proficiency possible, the standard language variety of wider communication used by the society as a whole" (p. 32).

The situation at Rogers Intermediate School was not perfect. Mistakes were made, and, in retrospect, there are things that the school administrators and teachers said they would likely do differently in terms of meeting Nitha and Bora's needs if they had the chance to start the school year over. Nonetheless, the efforts of the school appear to be consistent with Corson's principles outlined above. The teachers and staff showed respect for Nitha and Bora's native Khmer language, viewing it as a resource for learning rather than as a problem to be overcome (Ruiz, 1984). The teachers and staff were also determined to provide as much support as possible, using the resources they had within the school and community to help Nitha and Bora learn English and academic content to the highest levels possible.

The experience of Rogers Intermediate School has a number of implications for other teachers and their schools faced with similar challenges in meeting the language and educational needs of newly-arrived ELL students. The following implications represent lessons learned from this case study, and include recommendations for schools and teachers of newly-arrived ELL students, particularly when bilingual programs are not available or feasible:

- Differentiated classroom instruction – Newly-arrived ELLs with little to no English proficiency should not be expected to be able to fully participate in the classroom's regular, often assessment-driven instruction (Wright & Choi, 2005). ELLs require language and content-area instruction which is appropriate to their current proficiency in English and academic ability, and which is specially designed to help them attain higher levels of English proficiency and academic knowledge. In the academic literature, this is referred to as specially designed academic instruction in English (SDAIE) or "sheltered" instruction (Echevarria, 1998; Echevarria, Vogt, & Short, 2004; Peregoy & Boyle, 2004; Diaz-Rico & Weed, 2006). Such instruction does not mean that teachers lower their expectations for newly-arrived ELLs. Successful teachers of ELL students do have high expectations, but these expectations are reasonable, and teachers provide the means for their students to obtain them. Teachers need to plan separate but relevant lessons, classroom activities, and homework. They also need to structure their classroom time so that they can work individually with their ELL students on a daily basis.

• ESL instruction – In the best case scenario, the classroom teacher is certified to provide ESL instruction within her own classroom (Peregoy & Boyle, 2004). However, this is frequently not the case. Pull-out ESL is often viewed in a negative light as students may miss out on important content-area instruction in their classroom, and it is difficult for pull-out ESL teachers to coordinate their teaching relevant to instruction taking place in the regular classrooms (Ovando, Combs, & Collier, 2006).

Nonetheless, as shown in this study, pull-out ESL is a better option than leaving students in a mainstream classroom all day where they receive little personalized attention or instruction appropriate to their level. An experienced ESL teacher can provide much needed individualized language instruction, especially for newly-arrived ELLs, which accelerates their acquisition of English.

• Paraprofessionals – Paraprofessionals can provide much needed assistance for ELL students. They can assist teachers in delivering differentiated instruction. When they work with ELLs one-on-one or in small groups, they can create a supportive environment where students feel comfortable using their new language for communicative and academic purposes. Teachers should not expect their paraprofessionals to plan instruction for ELLs. Rather, teachers need to carefully plan lessons and select activities and materials for the paraprofessionals to use which supports and supplements regular classroom content-area instruction.

• Technology – When properly used, computers can provide an additional means of differentiating instruction, providing students access to material appropriate to their level, and providing ELL students with visual and audio support (Butler-Pascoe & Wiburg, 2003; Haley & Austin, 2003). Teachers should work with their school technology specialist to select software for use on classroom computers and/or in the computer lab which supplements classroom instruction in the language and content areas, which allows students to work at their own pace at a level appropriate to their language and academic proficiency level, and which provides ample scaffolding support enabling ELL students to successfully interact with and learn from the program.

• Primary language support – Students' native languages are not problems to be overcome, but a resource for learning language and academic content (Ruiz, 1984). Teachers should allow ELL students to use their native language in the classroom, as this helps to create a warm and welcoming environment conducive to learning a new language (Jesness, 2004; Ovando, Combs, & Collier, 2006; Wright, in press). When teachers allow and help students to use bilingual dictionaries, and allow students to talk to each other in their language, they enable their ELL students to complete work and learn new concepts and language they may not be able to otherwise (Echevarria, Vogt, & Short, 2004; Summers, 1988). When schools lack personnel who can speak students' native languages, teachers can turn to the community for help from volunteers who can come in to provide much needed primary language support.

Acknowledgements

This research was supported by a grant from the Academy for Teacher Excellence (ATE) at the University of Texas, San Antonio. I am most grateful to the faculty and staff of ATE for their encouragement and support of this study. I also wish to express my sincere gratitude to the dedicated teachers and staff at "Rodgers" Intermediate School, and most importantly to "Nitha" and "Bora" for their courage, hard work, and perseverance, for giving me the privilege to work with and learn from them, and for agreeing to participate in this study.

References

Adler, D., & Natti, S. (2002). *Cam Jansen and the birthday mystery*. New York: Puffin.

Ariza, E. N. W. (2006). *Not for ESOL teachers: What every classroom teacher needs to know about the linguistically, culturally, and ethnically diverse student*. Boston: Pearson/Allyn & Bacon.

Baker, C. (2001). *Foundations of bilingual education and bilingualism* (3rd ed.). Clevedon, England: Multilingual Matters.

Baker, C., & Jones, S. P. (1998). Submersion education. In C. Baker & S. P. Jones (Eds.), *Encyclopedia of bilingualism and bilingual education*. Clevedon, England: Multilingual Matters.

Beykont, Z. F. (Ed.). (2002). *The power of culture: Teaching across language differences*. Cambridge, MA: Harvard Education Publishing Group.

Butler-Pascoe, M. E., & Wiburg, K. M. (2003). *Technology and teaching English language learners*. Boston: Pearson/Allyn & Bacon.

Corson, D. (2001). *Language diversity and education*. Mahwah, NJ: Lawrence Erlbaum Associates, Publishers.

Crawford, J. (2004). *Educating English learners: Language diversity in the classroom* (5th ed.). Los Angeles: Bilingual Education Services, Inc.

Diaz-Rico, L. T., & Weed, K. Z. (2006). The cross-cultural, language, and academic development handbook: A complete K-12 reference guide (3rd ed.). Boston: Pearson/Allyn & Bacon.

Echevarria, J. (1998). *Teaching language minority students in elementary schools* (Research Brief #1). Santa Cruz, CA:

Center for Research on Education, Diversity & Excellence, University of California, Santa Cruz.

Echevarria, J. (2002). *Sheltered content instruction: Teaching English language learners with diverse abilities* (2nd ed.). Boston: Allyn & Bacon.

Echevarria, J., Vogt, M., & Short, D. (2004). *Making content comprehensible for English learners: The SIOP model* (2nd ed.). Boston: Pearson.

Erickson, F. (1986). Qualitative methods in research on teaching. In M. Wittrock (Ed.), *Handbook of research on teaching* (3rd ed.). New York: MacMillan.

Freeman, Y. S., & Freeman, D. E. (1998). *ESL/EFL teaching : Principles for success.* Portsmouth, NH: Heinemann.

Hadaway, N. L., Vardell, S. M., & Young, T. A. (2002). *Literature-based instruction with English language learners K-12.* Boston: Allyn & Bacon.

Haley, M. H., & Austin, T. Y. (2003). *Content-based second language teaching and learning: An interactive approach.* Boston: Allyn & Bacon.

Jesness, J. (2004). *Teaching English language learners K-12: A quick-start for the new teacher.* Thousand Oaks, CA: Corwin Press.

Krashen, S. D. (2003). *Explorations in language acquisition and use.* Portsmouth, NH: Heinemann.

Krashen, S. D. (1985). *The input hypothesis: Issues and implications.* London: Longman.

McNeil, L. M. (2000). *Contradictions of school reform: Educational costs of standardized testing.* New York: Routledge.

Lee, J. F., & Van Patten, B. (2003). *Making communicative language teaching happen* (2nd ed.). New York: Longman.

Miles, M. B., & Huberman, A. M. (1994). *Qualitative data analysis: An expanded sourcebook* (2nd ed.). Thousand Oaks, CA: Sage Publications.

Ministry of Education. (2004). *Cambodian education strategic plan 2004-2008*. Phnom Penh, Cambodia: Royal Government of Cambodia.

National Clearinghouse for English Language Acquisition. (2003, June). *The growing number of limited English proficient students 1992/93 - 2002/03.* Retrieved May 15, 2005, from http://www.ncela.gwu.edu/policy/states/reports/statedata/2002 LEP/Growing_LEP0203.pdf

Nation, I. S. P. (2001). *Learning vocabulary in another language.* Cambridge, UK: Cambridge University Press.

Ovando, C., Combs, M. C., & Collier, V. P. (2006). *Bilingual and ESL classrooms: Teaching in multicultural contexts* (4th ed.). Boston: McGraw Hill.

Peregoy, S. F., & Boyle, O. F. (2004). *Reading, writing and learning in ESL: A resource book for K-12 teachers* (4th ed.). Boston: Allyn & Bacon.

Peregoy, S. F., & Boyle, O. F. (2000). English learners reading English: What we know, what we need to know. *Theory into Practice (Special Issue: Children and Languages at School), 39*(4), 237-248.

Perez, B. (2003). *Becoming biliterate: A study of two-way bilingual immersion programs*. Mahwah, NJ: Lawrence Erlbaum Associates, Inc.

Pinnell, G. S., & Fountas, I. C. (1996). *Guided reading: Good first teaching for all children*. Portsmouth, NH: Heinemann.

Planning Department. (2006). *Education statistics and indicators (School year 01/02)*. Phnom Penh, Cambodia: Ministry of Education, Youth, and Sports.

Program Evaluation Unit. (2000). *The Texas successful schools study: Quality education for limited English proficient students*. Austin, TX: Texas Education Agency. Available: http://www.ncela.gwu.edu/pubs/tea/tsss.pdf.

Ruiz, R. (1984). Orientations in language planning. *NABE - The Journal of the National Association for Bilingual Education,* *8*(2), 15-34.

Schmitt, N. (2000). *Vocabulary in language teaching.* Cambridge, UK: Cambridge University Press.

Shapiro, N., & Adelson-Goldstein, J. (1999). *The Oxford picture dictionary: English/Cambodian.* New York: Oxford University Press.

Summers, D. (1988). The role of dictionaries in language learning. In R. Carter & M. McCarthy (Eds.), *Vocabulary and language teaching.* New York: Longman.

Tripp, V. (1999). *Do you like my pet?* Carmel, CA: Hampton Brown Books.

Um, K. (1999). Scars of war: Educational issues and challenges for Cambodian-American students. In C. C. Park & M. M.-Y. Chi (Eds.), *Asian-American education: Prospects and challenges* (pp. 263-284). Westport, CT: Bergin & Garvey.

Valenzuela, A. (2004). *Leaving children behind: How "Texas-style" accountability fails Latino youth.* New York: State University of New York Press.

Wiley, T. G., & Wright, W. E. (2004). Against the undertow: The politics of language instruction in the United States. *Educational Policy, 18*(1), 142-168.

Wright, W. E. (in press). Primary language support: Using ELL students' native language(s) to make English more comprehensible. *TX TESOL Newsletter.*

Wright, W. E. (2005). *Evolution of federal policy and implications of No Child Left Behind for language minority students* (No. EPSL-0501-101-LPRU). Tempe, AZ: Language Policy Research Unit, Education Policy Studies Laboratory, Arizona State University. Available: http://www.asu.edu/educ/epsl/EPRU/documents/EPSL-0501-101-LPRU.pdf.

Wright, W. E. (2004). What English-only really means: A study of
    the implementation of California language policy with
    Cambodian American students. *International Journal of
    Bilingual Education and Bilingualism, 7*(1), 1-23.
Wright, W. E., & Choi, D. (2005). *Voices from the classroom: A
    statewide survey of experienced third-grade English language
    learner teachers on the impact of language and high-stakes
    testing policies in Arizona.* Tempe, AZ: Educational Policy
    Studies Laboratory, Arizona State University. Available:
    http://www.asu.edu/educ/epsl/EPRU/documents/EPSL-0512-
    104-LPRU.pdf.

---

[1] "Khmer" and "Cambodian" are frequently used interchangeably to refer to both the people and their language. In this paper, I use Khmer (pronounced by native speakers as Khmai) to refer to the language, and Cambodian to refer to the people.

Children's Literature: Validating and Valuing Language and Culture

Janelle Mathis
University of North Texas

The significant role of children's literature in the ESL classroom has been acknowledged for more than a decade by scholars, and many teachers have realized its value for even longer. Since the landmark study by Larrick (1965) that pointed to the lack of representation of children from diverse ethnicities in children's and adolescent literature, a growing concern exists for both the accurate portrayal of children from many cultures as well as an increase in the number of titles that authentically reflects the growing diversity of society. Multicultural and multiethnic literature has become increasingly available for all grade levels, and the conversations around the criteria for excellent authentic books extend beyond that of avoiding stereotypes to the ongoing dialogue of authors, publishers, scholars, and professional organizations around specific topics, such as: Who can write for what culture? How much "truth" is required to be authentic? How accurate is the use of a second language within a book? and What engagements will extend the insights into this book?

Awards have been created to acknowledge significant literary contributions that represent specific cultural groups. For example, through the American Library Association, the Coretta Scott King award is presented yearly to an African American author and an illustrator for outstanding books that promote cultural understanding and the realization of the American dream. The Pura Belpré Award, established in 1996, is presented to a Latino/Latina writer and illustrator whose outstanding work best portrays, affirms, and celebrates the Latino cultural experience. The Batchelder Award is given to an American publisher for an exceptional children's book originally published in a foreign language in a foreign country and subsequently translated into English. Various professional organizations recognize particular groups of outstanding cultural books. Selected by a committee from the Children's Literature Special Interest Group of the International Reading Association, the Notable Books for a Global Society is a group of 25 books published each year that enhance student understanding of people and cultures throughout the world. The National Council of Social Studies with the Children's Book Council provides a yearly list of Notable Social Studies Trade Books for Young People each year framed around the thematic strands of the NCSS curriculum standards.

Yet, despite great strides in the creation and recognition of multicultural literature, the amount of literature published still does not meet the needs of a population whose demographics speak to the reality of cultural pluralism, nor does the literature address specifically the distinctive cultural groups within each of the more widely acknowledged and under-represented cultural and linguistic groups. These gaps will be filled only as educators recognize the potential of literature and insist on greater publication of a diversity of titles to meet curriculum mandates and the needs of ESL learners.

In today's social and political educational climate, and in light of the instructional issues described in other chapters of this document, the potential of children's and adolescent literature in the classroom is even greater than previously documented or imagined. Linguistics research points to important implications for reading instruction and material (Christianson, 2002). Likewise, sociocultural perspectives of instruction speak loudly to the role of multicultural literature as both a window and a mirror (Sims-Bishop, 1982), validating the life experiences of those whose culture is reflected and creating insights for others to view people and events in society much different from themselves. In the hands of an instructor sensitive to the needs of the whole child, such literature coupled with engaging strategies can provide ESL learners with pathways to enhanced identity, increased awareness and sensitivity to those who share a community, demonstrations of powerful uses of language for a variety of purposes, and the potential for developing critical literacy and taking stances on social issues within the local and larger communities of which young readers are a part (Gollnick & Chin, 1994; Nieto, 1997; Nilsson, 2006). The present discussion is based on the belief that instruction for ESL learners must acknowledge and validate all aspects of the learner's cultural identity of which language is an inseparable part.

With the growing number of titles that are published, it might prove a daunting task to identify the many books which, while not necessarily culture-specific, can prove potentially empowering for readers. However, if one considers categories that align with the current scholarship in the field of ESL children's literature and with the potential outcomes of excellent, authentic literature stated in the above paragraph, a variety of literature emerges that can, throughout the curriculum, provide empowering cultural and literacy experiences for English language learners. The four categories below are used to assist in organizing and emphasizing the rich possibilities of certain books. While the titles listed within each category are fluid and one title often exemplifies several significant characteristics of a good book for ESL learners, they are organized to better enable this discussion and the contemplation of the potential of children's literature. Some of the titles here will, no doubt, be familiar, while others purposely draw attention to more recent publications. Potential strategies point to the importance of reading aloud, valuing individual voices, negotiating meaning through discussion, and responding through a variety of sign systems, such as drama, music, and art. Within limited space, various titles are described, although at the conclusion of this chapter is a sampling of recent chapter and picture books that are excellent representatives of each category. Since for every award winner, or suggested title within an article such as this, numerous other books are also published that are powerful resources, it is hoped that the suggestions here are compelling invitations for teachers to become involved in learning more about current children's and adolescent literature.

Literature reflecting the cultural identities of the learner to include language

Books that reflect the varied experiences of diverse learners are found within all genres and reflect life experiences of all age levels. Cultural traditions to include ethnic foods, celebrations, music, dance, and art, as well as family and society day-to-day events are often portrayed eloquently, inviting a reader's response to shared life experiences. While it is obvious that children enjoy reading and hearing about the worlds beyond their own culture, all individuals have the need for validation by others—to see their lives represented in books for all to read. Realizing that other characters, both fictional and real, have stories of success, humor, resiliency, and challenges, readers develop a sense of possibility, confidence, and community. Often these characters depict problem solving and hopeful spirits as well as cleverness and pride that transfers when readers identify with them.

Using the home cultures of ESL learners helps to create the critical bridge, addressed frequently in professional literature, between what is valued and useful at home and at school. "Schooling isn't about moving from one world to another but about transforming worlds through shared, complex journeys" (Van Sluys & Riener, 2006, p. 322). One might add to this notion that children's literature can be vehicles in this transforming journey.   Using culturally relevant literature can provide a compelling reason to use language—to share one's personal connections with others and have a voice in discussions around familiar topics. Parents can be involved as well in exploring, enjoying, and critiquing books that represent specific aspects of their culture. One strategy to extending reading might be to use culturally relevant literature as models for families to create their own cultural books to share in the classroom.

A Song for Ba (Yee, 2004) takes place in the early twentieth century and is about a young boy whose father and grandfather sing in the Chinese opera. This form of opera uses only men and for the immigrants to North American in this story, it is their livelihood as well as a cultural tradition to maintain at a time when other forms of entertainment are becoming more popular. Ba learns how to sing the female roles from his grandfather and is able to help when his father must assume the female role. The story informs of both this cultural aspect as well as the hardships of Chinese immigrants at this time. *Shanghai Messenger* (Cheng, 2005) is a more contemporary story about a young girl who makes a trip in the opposite direction--from Ohio to Shanghai--to visit her extended family for the first time. The poignant free-verse format shares not only the significance of her visit for the whole family, but readers receive much information about China through the eyes of this eleven-year-old traveler. The situation is one that most likely will resonate within an ESL class. Pam Muñoz Ryan writes books filled with cultural connections. In *Becoming Naomi Leon* (2005), Naomi and her brother are living with her great grandmother when her mother, described as irresponsible, returns with her boyfriend. Naomi travels to Oaxaca to find her father for his signature on paperwork making Gram her legal guardian. Both cultural insights and the theme of family love and security are obvious connections for readers.

Language is perhaps the most critical cultural aspect to maintain and develop as it is the essence of identity, maintaining and connecting the other facets of culture to each other and to the individual. Linguistically speaking, the role of a child's native language in the development of the second language is acknowledged. "First languages, however, are more than a means to second-language learning; they are inseparable from a child's identity and culture. When we restrict or prohibit the use of first languages in classrooms, we are asking children to choose between home and school cultures and are wasting incredible linguistic and cultural resources that would enrich classroom life and learning" (Short, Schroeder, Kauffman, & Kaser, 2006, p. 287).

Numerous other reasons attest to using literature that is partially or completely in a student's first language. When considering the notion of *language as resource*, children's literature can provide exemplary demonstrations of other languages besides English in use in the daily lives of children whose first language is not English. Literature that is inclusive of a variety of languages creates a context of inclusiveness insofar as ". . . it highlights the interests of the entire society rather than those of particular minority groups and, in so doing, transcends the 'us versus them' mentality that characterizes much of the debate in this area" (Ruiz, 1988, p. 299). And, Nilsson has noted that, "Empirical research, such as Rosberg's (1995) study of native-English-speaking and bilingual children who were exposed to multicultural books written in different languages, has suggested such books can help children develop greater awareness and appreciation of the features of diverse languages" (p. 535).

Literature in the learner's first language has numerous benefits. It encourages readers to use their first language more meaningfully in oral and written forms as they access their prior knowledge through their first language while building meaning in their second. They also have the opportunity to become the expert when literature is used that contains their first language. One middle school student who, according to his teacher, rarely said a word became suddenly interested, involved, and articulate when he was positioned as the person with the knowledge of Spanish pronunciation while reading George Ancona's (1998) *Fiesta Fireworks* (Mathis, 2002). Non-English-speaking parents can enjoy reading stories to their children in their own language and expand on the ideas, values, skills, and concepts they encounter in the books. Through the use of audiocassettes of literature, ESL students and parents are exposed to English vocabulary in addition to common grammatical structures and conventions.

Books inclusive of the Spanish language are limited but easily found, especially when examining the books from smaller presses. *Magda's Tortillas* (Chavarria-Chairez, 2000) is a story about a young seven-year-old girl whose grandmother is teaching her to make tortillas for her birthday. In both Spanish and English readers enjoy the story of Magda's unsuccessful efforts to make perfectly round tortillas as well as the memories that her loving grandmother finds in the varied shapes of Magda's initial efforts. The story is told in both English and Spanish with some Spanish phrases used in the dialogue between characters within the English version. This typical family scene produces much dialogue among children as they read or hear it read aloud. *Uncle Rain Cloud* (Johnston, 2001) contains numerous words in Spanish within the text in this typical scenario of a young boy who must translate for his uncle, much to the frustration of Tío Tomás. The story sends the message of valuing two cultures and ends with Carlos teaching his uncle English and Uncle Tomas teaching Carlos the Spanish stories of the tongue-twister gods from Mexico folklore.

While books in languages other than Spanish are not as easily found, interesting and authentic titles do exist. *In the Leaves* (Lee, 2005) introduces Mandarin Chinese characters here, as the main character shows his friends the characters he knows. As with *In the Park* (Lee, 1998), the author uses simple, descriptive text and dialogue to support meaning and to create a context for each of the characters. Using nature's settings to describe the language is quite a natural way to learn since art and life are both elements of how the characters are constructed. *Sequoyah, the Cherokee Man Who Gave His People Writing* (Rumford, 2005) is an excellent resource for all readers as it tells the biography of this famous Native American and contains parallel text in Cherokee. This demonstration of Sequoyah's ultimate life's work is a valuable resource for all readers but especially Cherokee children who know their native language.

Literature reflecting universal themes found in all cultures

Many books focus on universal topics or themes and provide points of connection for all readers. Themes such as family, friends, celebrations, school, or food provide topics to which even the youngest of readers can connect and have points of comparison to share with others. More abstract themes, while often especially appealing to the social and emotional development of older readers, are powerful ways to focus on literature at all grade levels. Topics such as identity, conflict, developing relationships, a sense of place, or even social justice are issues found in all cultures and books with themes on these topics help literacy learners as they develop a vocabulary for talking about issues; articulate personal opinions through comparison, examples, justification, and other means of developing voice; negotiate with others the varied meanings of such themes; and build personal identity as part of the larger society with whom they share these universal themes.

Often the book's focus is that of gathering a variety of information from different cultures around a certain topic. In *A life like mine, how children live around the world* (UNICEF, 2002), readers find many points of comparison among a diversity of life styles. Based on the Convention on the Rights of the Child, this photographic essay documents the fundamental rights of all children. Focusing on children around the world, how they live, and what they need to be happy and healthy, this book is arranged around four main sections -- "Survival," "Development," "Protection," and "Participation." It also shares how children express themselves in different ways, as well as both the hardships and joys they endure in a variety of societies. A discussion about the United Nations "Rights" also offers valuable insights and opportunities for multilingual classroom discussions. *Let's Eat* (2004) focuses on five children around the world who have very different ideas about what makes a good meal, but each actively takes part in shopping, cooking, and celebrating mealtime with their families. These are two of many titles that are framed around common themes that point to universal activities, needs, and concepts among cultures. Each offers great points of discussion and invites language use around personal experiences.

Many teachers employ Cinderella variants as they consider universal themes in many cultures. With literally hundreds of variants that resemble this European fairytale, students enjoy comparing literary elements, motifs, and culturally specific elements including language for each version. Frequently, they will recognize a story from their own culture and become the expert in telling how it is alike or different from the version they know. A recent ESL middle school student who immigrated from

Thailand was in a reading class where *Yeh-Shen, a Cinderella story from China* (Louie, 1982) was read along with other variants. He immediately recognized the story and shared in English his experience winning a storytelling contest for his rendition of *Yeh-Shen* (Mathis, 2002). Books that reflect universal themes and topics invite readers to share their stories as well through writing and oral language.

The *Hickory Chair* (Faustino, 2001) is about the relationship between a young boy and his grandmother. Although he is blind, the child is never described through his disability, even though his blindness is part of the story's plot when he must find notes left in favorite hiding places by his grandmother after her death that tell family members what she left for each of them. Readers can relate to this relationship and to objects they may have that represent a story in their lives. For older readers, *The Story of My Life* (Ahmedi, 2005) offers a chance to think about facing challenges and resiliency as this true autobiographical story relates a young immigrant's experience of losing her leg as a result of a landmine in Afghanistan. Told simplistically but powerfully from a high school student's perspective, this story shares her life now in the U.S. after this tragedy over a decade ago. Both overcoming obstacles and dealing with coming to a new culture are themes that can elicit conversation and writing.

Literature as demonstrations of language conventions, rich vocabulary, and authentic uses of language

Children's literature is an excellent demonstration of language for all readers. The repetitive language and story concepts, the unique organizational strategies, the predictable and/or cumulative story traits, the visual support within picture books, and rhythm and rhyme of poetry are only some of the literary qualities that provide language experiences that support ESL learners. While many books demonstrate these traits and bring delightful demonstrations of the unique qualities of language to all readers, some significant examples blend both multicultural characteristics and exemplary language.

As an exemplar book that is culturally specific, *José! Born to Dance* (Reich, 2005) provides great examples of sensory imagery. This story of the great choreographer José Limón, who fled Mexico to California during the Mexican Revolution, is rich in the artistic use of words as well as color. Sounds from lullabies, bullfights, and flamenco dances are evident in the text and influenced José's eventual dance movements. Spanish words are throughout (and defined both in text and at the end). This is also a story of determination as José reacts to being teased in school for poor English and perseveres to become a dancer and choreographer. The imagery and rhythm represent great examples of fluency in language use for delightful reading. The arts are also the focus in *The Pot that Juan Built* (Andrews-Goebel, 2002). The cumulative format of this highly interesting story about a famous pottery maker in Mexico follows the pattern of the traditional narrative poem, *The House that Jack Built*. In addition to the precise use of words within this poetic format, informational text and brightly colored illustrations further explain each stanza throughout the process of creating the pottery.

In *My Diary from Here to There / Mi Diario de Aquí Hasta Allá* (Pérez, 2002), readers receive an example of literacy used for a functional purpose—to keep a diary. This book is also a good example of dual language and serves to show the role of writing within one's personal life. *Bronx Masquerade* (Grimes, 2002) provides another example of writing for authentic purpose. In this novel, a high school class discovers the power of poetry to share their own identity. Each chapter focuses on a different character from diverse backgrounds in an inner city high school and the rich character descriptions provide excellent insight into language use from a high school perspective.

Literature as opportunities for critical literacy around social issues

Literacy teachers today are concerned with not only teaching the processes of reading and writing, but also with teaching learners to take a critical stance as they make meaning from text. They often encourage readers to adopt a questioning stance and to work toward changing themselves and their world. Often these notions of critical literacy are focused on issues of equity and democracy and are supported with examples in all genres in children's literature. It is not enough that students read about these issues. To develop a critical stance toward both the information read and the issues therein, teachers need to engage students in thoughtful discussions and inquiry. In a study of bilingual first grade children participating in literature discussion groups around books that focused on social issues, Martinez-Roldán (2005) found "the groups provided a context for students to engage in literary talk about texts while listening and considering each others' voices and perspectives regardless of individual reading proficiency or language dominance" (p. 25). The author points to the role of discussion around books as evidence of Vygotsky's sociocultural and historical theory that provides an account of learning and development as a mediated process. Martinez-Roldán states:

> He attributed a major role in development to social, cultural, and historical factors and proposed that cultural and psychological tools (i.e., language, works of art, writing) and other human beings (i.e., teachers, peers) mediate children's thinking and learning. Culture and community are not just factors that impact learning; they are, as several scholars have pointed out, the mediational means through which ideas are developed. (p. 29).

Literature represents a significant "psychological" tool through which thinking and learning are mediated. Martinez-Roldán also articulates the important notion that participation in the social construction of meaning and critical thinking should not wait until students develop specific language or reading skills to facilitate critical discussions and inquiry talk. Van Sluys and Reiner (2006) in a study focusing ESL learners' multiple ways of knowing in multilingual classroom communities stated, "Literacy learners need places that recognize how literacy learning is intimately tied to identity and how becoming literate involves a range of practices including critical practices for reading words and worlds" (p.327).

Many books have recently been published that provide points of discussion around current and historical social issues. Picture books use illustration to help communicate the story and are excellent resources for readers of all ages. Chapter books, while one needs to consider developmentally appropriate criteria, consists of numerous titles that provide excellent vehicles for ongoing contemplation around various issues. While chapter books might offer more text that some ESL learners can efficiently tackle, reading aloud at all grade levels has an extensive research basis that speaks to language development inclusive of reading, writing, speaking, and listening (Moss, 2006). We also know that a learning community is being formed when a group that is sharing the same story within the same context provides fertile grounds for the social construction of knowledge through dialogue.

Playing War (Beckwith, 2005) is a simple story but powerful in the message it bears. Luke and his friends decide one hot afternoon to play "war." Sameer is new to the neighborhood and decides not to play since he has experienced a real war in which his house was destroyed and a family member killed. The young boys are surprised at his story and respond sensitively, thus providing a potential vehicle in this book for discussing the impact of war. *Henry and the Kite Dragon* (Hall, 2004) takes place in the early 1900's and focuses on a conflict between children in Chinatown and Little Italy in New York City. Henry and Grandfather Chin make beautiful kites that are flown frequently in the neighborhood but they are often destroyed by nearby Italian boys. After discovering that the kites scare the pet pigeons of the Italians, the two groups are able to peacefully agree on a solution. Cultural understanding and peaceful negotiating are both central to this plot. Yet another type of critical thinking around a social issue is invited in response to Uhlberg's (2005), *Dad, Jackie Robinson and Me*. Taking place in 1947, the author and his deaf father spend the summer following Jackie Robinson at a time when the racial prejudice was strong against this black baseball player. The deaf father identifies with Jackie and his struggle for respect. This book offers many insights into this time in US history as well as the notions of prejudice affecting many different aspects of culture.

Before We Were Free (Alvarez, 2002) is a book for adolescent readers that focuses on what life might be like for a teenager living under a dictatorship in the Dominican Republic. The tension, fear, and political and civil unrest are met with courage by a family who does not flee but remains to make a difference. Such strength of character may provide numerous connections for readers.

Drama strategies are also a means for ESL learners to engage in critical meaning making around issues of social justice. Medina and Campano (2006) describe two classrooms in which writing and process drama were used with ESL fifth graders in creating spaces for critical literacy experiences. Their work supports the belief here that various strategies such as tableau, creating original dialogue, or assuming differing points of view, can help to connect the reader's life experiences to literature, build identities, construct knowledge, and ultimately develop language understandings as students navigate between their first and second languages. Dramatic response to texts maintains the empowering potential of literature.

Who Will Tell My Brother? (Carvel, 2004) is about Evan, a Native American youth, who, in learning more about his heritage, ancestors, and culture, asks his school to do away with the degrading school Indian mascot that calls up the distasteful paper headdresses, tomahawks, whoops, and racial stereotypes. No one will stand behind him and the half Mohawk teen must face ostracism, bullying, and eventually violence. This lesson in integrity and courage might involve students through process drama as they take the role of others in the scenario who might be for or against Evan. Physically positioning themselves can also involve a verbal or written experience as they justify their beliefs. Letters can be written to the school board and a hearing could be held that involves parents, teachers, and students. Tableau or pantomime might be ways of showing the emotional tension of Evan and others. This powerful book can be even more powerful as readers consider "what if" they were part of this community.

Conclusion

The suggestions here are but an invitation to encourage educators to explore more deeply the diversity of authors, genres, formats, and topics as they nurture the literacy development of ESL learners. It is also hoped that as ESL teachers discover new titles that reach the hearts and minds of their students, they share these titles, their students' responses, and any powerful strategies that evolved. Through enthusiastic discussions with colleagues, contributing to professional journals, or presenting at conferences, sharing--endorsing through example--the significant role of children's literature in the ESL classroom sends messages to authors, publishers, and educators in all positions.

We know that literacy is not merely decoding or the transmission of knowledge and that the complexities of literacy learning are enriched by the cultural diversity that young readers bring to the reading event. We know that literacy itself is assuming new identities, often through technology and globalization, within the descriptors of "new literacies," "sign systems," and "critical literacy." As educators throughout the various content areas, we owe it to our ESL students to create learning environments that call upon their "funds of knowledge" (Moll, 2001) as they delve, along with their classmates, into critical and creative thinking. Children's and adolescent literature support and contribute to such an environment.

Resources for the classroom

Literature reflecting the cultural experiences of the learner to include language

Ancona, G. (1998). *Fiesta fireworks*. New York: Harper Collins.

Argueta, J. (2005). *Moony luna, luna, lunita lunera*. San Francisco: Children's Book Press.

Bercaw, E. C. (2000). *Halmoni's day*. New York: Dial.

Bertrand, D. G. (1999). *Trino's choice*. Houston: Arte Publico Press.

Bertrand, D. G. (1995). *Sweet fifteen*. Houston; Arte Publico Press.

Brown, M. (2004). *My name is Celia / Me llamo Celia: The life of Celia Cruz / La vida de Celia Cruz*. Flagstaff, AZ: Luna Rising (a bilingual imprint of Northland Publishing).

Canales, V. (2005). *The tequila worm.* New York: Wendy Lamb Books (a division of Random House).

Carvell, M. (2005). *Sweetgrass basket*. New York: Dutton.

Chavarria-Chairez, B. (2000). *Magda's tortillas*. Houston: Arte Publico Press.

Cheng, S. (2005). *Shanghai messenger*. New York: Lee & Low.

Choi, Y. (2001). *The name jar*. New York: Knopf Books for Young Readers.

Compestine, Y. C. (2006). *D is for dragon dance*. New York: Holiday House.

Delecre, L. (2000). *Salsa stories*. New York: Scholastic.

Gallo, D. R. (Ed). (2004). *First crossing, stories about teen immigrants*. Cambridge, MA: Candlewick Press.

Garza, C. L. (1990, 2005). *Family pictures*. San Francisco, CA: Children's Book Press.

Johnston, T. (2001). *Uncle Rain Cloud*. Watertown, ME: Charlesbridge.

Kyuchukov, H. (2004). *My name was Hussein*. Honesdale, PA: Boyds Mills Press.

Lee, H. V. (2005). *In the leaves*. New York: Henry Holt.

Lee, H. V. (1998). *In the park*. New York: Henry Holt.

Mora, P. (2005). *Doña Flor: A tall tale about a giant woman with a great big heart*. New York: Alfred A. Knopf (a division of Random House).

Orozco, Jose-Luis. (2005). *Rin, rin, rin / do, re, mi*. New York: Orchard Books.

Park, L. S. (2005). *Bee-bim bop!* New York: Clarion.

Reich, S. (2005). *Jose! born to dance*. New York: Simon & Schuster.

Rumford, J. (2004). *Sequoyah, the Cherokee man who gave his people writing*. Boston: Houghton Mifflin.

Ryan, P. M. (2005). *Becoming Naomi Leon*. New York: Scholastic.

Wing, N. (1996). *Jalapeno bagels*. New York: Atheneum.

Yee, P. (2004). *A song for Ba*. Toronto, Canada: Groundwood Books.

Yolen, J. (1992). *Street rhymes*. Honesdale, PA: Boyds Mills Press.

Literature reflecting universal themes found in all cultures

Amedi, F., & Ansari, T. (2005). *The story of my life*. New York: Simon & Schuster.

Ada, A.F., & Savadier, E. (2002) *I love saturdays y domingos*. New York: Atheneum (Simon and Schuster).

Ajmera, M., & Ivanko, J.D. (1999). *To be a kid*. Watertown, MA: Charlesbridge.

Aliki. (1998). *Marianthe's story one: Painted words / Marianthe's story two: Spoken memories.* New York: Greenwillow.

Birdseye, D. H.,& Birdseye, T. (1997). *Under our skin*. New York: Holiday House.

Fox, M. (1984). *Wilfrid Gordon McDonald Partridge*. New York: Kane Miller.

Fraustino, L. R. (2001). *The hickory chair*. New York: Scholastic.

Harrington, J. N. (2004). *Going north*. New York: Farrar, Straus, Giroux.

Hollyer, B. (20040. *Let's eat*. New York: Henry Holt.

Kuklin, S. (2006). *Families*. New York: Hyperion.

Lacapa, M. (1994). *Less than half, more than whole*. Flagstaff, AZ: Northland.

Louie, (1982). *Yeh-Shen, a Cinderella story from China*. New York: Penguin.

Medina, J. (1999). *My Name is Jorge, on both sides of the river: Poems in English and Spanish*. Honesdale, PA: Boyds Mills Press.

Morris, A. (1998). *Work*. New York: Lothrop, Lee, & Shepard.

Morris, A. (1998). *Play*. New York: Lothrop, Lee, & Shepard.

Radunsky, V. (2004). *What does peace feel like?* New York: Simon & Schuster.

Rosa-Casanova. S. *(1997). Mama Provi and the pot of rice*. New York: Atheneum.

Singer, M. (Ed.). (2004). *Face relations: 11 stories about seeing beyond color*. New York: Simon & Schuster.

UNICEF (2002). *A life like mine, how children live around the world?* New York: Dorling-Kindersley.

Literature as demonstrations of language conventions, rich vocabulary, and authentic uses of language

Ada, A. F. (1997). *Gathering the sun, an alphabet in Spanish and English*. New York: Lothrop, Lee, & Shepard.

Begay, S. (1995). *Voices and visions across the mesa*. New York: Scholastic.

Bruchac. J. (2005). *Code talker: A novel about the Navajo marines of World War Two*. New York: Dial.

Andrews-Goebel, N. (2002). *The pot that Juan built*. New York: Lee & Low.

Carlson, L. M. Ed. (2005). *Red hot salsa, bilingual poems on being young and Latino in the United States.* New York: Henry Holt.

Grimes, N. (2002). *Bronx masquerade.* New York: Dial Books for Young Readers.

King, M. L., Jr. (1997*). I have a dream.* New York: Scholastic.

Krudwig, V.L. (1998). *Cucumber soup.* Golden, CO: Fulcrum Publishing.

Morales, Y. (2003). *Just a minute: A trickster tale and counting book.* San Francisco: Chronicle Books.

Nye, N. S. (1999). *What have you lost?* New York: Greenwillow.

Orozco, J.L. (Ed.). (2004). *Fiestas: A year of Latin American songs of celebration.* New York: Penguin Young Readers.

Pérez, A.I. (2002). *My diary from here to there / Mi diario de aqui hasta alla.* San Franciso: Children's Book Press.

Ryan, P. M. (2001). *Mice and beans.* New York: Scholastic Press.

Soto, G. (1997). *Chato's kitchen.* New York: Putnam Juvenile.

Wong, J. S. (1999). *Behind the wheel, poems about driving.* New York: Simon & Schuster.

Wood, D. (2004). *A quiet place.* New York: Simon & Schuster.

Literature as opportunities for critical literacy around social issues

Alvarez, Julia. (2002). *Before we were free.* New York:

Random House.

Beckwith, K. (2005). *Playing war.* Gardiner, ME: Tilsbury House.

Bernier-Grand, C. (2005). *Cesar: ¡Sí, se puede! = Yes, we can!* Singapore: Marshall Cavendish Children's Books.

Bridges, R. (1999). *Through my eyes.* New York: Scholastic.

Carvell, M. (2004). *Who will tell my brother?* New York: Hyperion.

Fleming, C. (2003). *Boxes for Katje.* New York: Farrar, Straus and Giroux.

Giovanni, N. (2005). *Rosa.* New York: Henry Holt.

Hall, B.E. (2004). *Henry and the kite dragon.* New York: Philomel/Penguin Young Readers Group.

Singer, M. (Ed.). (2004*). Face relations: 11 stories about seeing beyond color.* New York: Simon & Schuster.

Smith, D.J. (2002). *If the world were a village: A book about the world's people.* Tonawando, NY: Kids Can Press.

Staples, S. F. (2005). *Under the persimmon tree.* New York: Farrar, Straus, Giroux.

Uhlberg, M. (2005). *Dad, Jackie Robinson and me.* Atlanta, GA: Peachtree.

Woodsen, J. (2001). *The other side.* New York: Penguin Putnam.

References

Christianson, D. (2002). *Language use in multiethnic literature for young adults.* Mount Pleasant: Central Michigan University. (ERIC Document Reproduction Service No. ED477555)

Gollnick, D.M., & Chinn, P.C. (1994). *Multicultural education in a pluralistic society.* New York: Merrill.

Larrick, N. (1965, September 11). The all-white world of children's books. *Saturday Review, 48*, 63-65, 84-85.

Martinez-Rodán, C. M. (2005). The inquiry acts of bilingual children in literature discussion. *Language Arts, 3*, 22-32.

Medina, C.L., & Campano, G. (2006). Performing identities through drama and teatro practices in multilingual classrooms. *Language Arts 83*, 332-341.

Moll, L. C. (2001). The diversity of schooling: A cultural-historical approach. In M. de la Luz Reyes & J. J. Halcón (Eds.), *The best for our children: Critical perspectives on literacy for Latino students* (pp. 13–28). New York: Teachers College Press.

Mathis, J. (2002). An album of response: Reflecting on the images. *Journal of Children's Literature, 28*(1), 41-46.

Moss, J. F. (2006). *Literature, literacy & comprehension strategies in the elementary school.* Urbana, IL: National Council of Teachers of English.

Nieto, S. (1997). We have stories to tell: Pueito Ricans in children's books. In V.J. Harris (Ed.), *Using multiethnic literature in the K–8 classroom* (pp. 59–93). Norwood, MA: Christopher-Gordon.

Nilsson, N. L. (2005). How does Hispanic portrayal in children's books measure up after 40 years? *The Reading Teacher, 58*, 534-548.

Ruiz, R. (1988). Orientations in language planning. In S. McKay and S. L. Wong (Eds.), *Language diversity: Problem or resource?* (pp. 3–25). New York: Newbury House.

Short, K., Schroeder, J., Kauffman, G., & Kaser, S. (2006). Thoughts from the editors. *Language Arts, 83,* 287.

Sims - Bishop, R. (1982). *Shadow and substance.* Urbana, IL: National Council of Teachers of English.

Van Sluys, K. and Reiner, R. (2006). Seeing the possibilities: Learning from, with, and about multilingual classroom communities. *Language Arts*, 83, 321-331.

Hispanic Oral Tradition: An Untapped Resource for Promoting Language Development

Claudia Sanchez
Texas Woman's University

Introduction

A popular saying in Spanish states, *"Lo que bien se aprende, nunca se olvida"* ("That which one learns well, one never forgets") and I have found this to be very true in my career as a professional educator. Growing up in Mexico as the oldest of four daughters in a middle class family, it was through playing with family and friends that I acquired much of the Hispanic oral tradition – the knowledge, values, attitudes, customs my culture transmits from generation to generation through the spoken word. As a child, television was restricted to one hour per day and videogames (which were nowhere near the sophisticated gadgets found today) were a rare weekend pastime. The only explanation my sisters and I got for the restricted times of television and videogame fun was that "a few minutes is enough and you do not *need* any more than that."

With television and videogames seriously limited at home, my sisters and I had to become creative in finding alternative ways to entertain ourselves. Thanks to this necessity, many years later, I discovered my love for my native language and the Hispanic oral tradition. As a result, I am a firm advocate for the preservation of Hispanic oral traditions and incorporate some of its forms, namely, theater-like play based on traditional children's songs, riddles, *dichos* or popular sayings, *rondas* or circle games and songs, and *trabalenguas* or tongue twisters into my teaching even today.

Children's theater

As a child, I had plenty of opportunities to listen to the radio. My favorite songs were those that told stories – like those by *Cri-cri*, the *Grillito Cantor* (Singing Grasshopper). *Cri-Cri*'s songs told stories for children. These stories always started and ended with its well-known theme, el *Tema de Cri-Cri* (Cri-Cri´s Theme).

¿Quién es ese que anda ahí?	Who is that over there?
¡Es Cri-Cri! ¡Es Cri-Cri!	It's *Cri- Cri*, it's *Cri-Cri!*
¿Y quien es ese Señor?	And who is that gentleman?
¡El grillo cantor!	The singing grasshopper!
¿Quién es el que anduvo ahí?	Who was that over here?
¡Fue Cri-Cri, Fue Cri-Cri!	It was *Cri-Cri*, it was *Cri-Cri!*
¿Y quien es ese Señor?	And who is that gentleman?
¡El grillo cantor!	The singing grasshopper!

The following are the lyrics of *Cri-Cri*'s song called *¿Cómo le va?* (How do you do?, Soler, 1945 as cited by De la Colina, Helguera, García, García, García, Hinojosa, et al., 1999) that tells a story about how a squirrel called *señora Ardilla* greets her friends in the woods and starts conversations with them. An English translation is presented below, although it should be noted that the

Spanish lyrics do incorporate rhyme and rhythm that the English version does not.

"¿Cómo le va?"	**"How are you doing?"**
Corre que te corre, pizpireta	Hopping, and hopping, such a lively lady
siempre tan coqueta	always so pretty,
para poner atención	ready to pay attention,
cuando en su camino	when in her way
se presenta la ocasión	there is an opportunity
de entablar conversación	to start a conversation.
¿Cómo le va, señor Venado?	How are you doing, Mr. Deer?
¿Cómo le va, qué tal ha estado?	How have you been?
Espero en Dios	I hope you are doing very well,
que esté usted muy bien,	and your dad and your mom, as
y su papá y su mamá también.	well.
¿Cómo le va, señora Ardilla?	How are you doing, Mrs. Squirrel?
¡Qué linda está con su sombrilla!	You look so pretty with your umbrella!
Cuénteme usted, ¿alguna novedad?	Tell me, what's new?
¿Cómo le va?	How are you doing?
¿Cómo le va?	How are you doing?
¿Cómo le va?	How are you doing?
¿Cómo le va, Señor Conejo?	How are you doing, Mr. Rabbit?
Usted jamás se pone viejo	You always look so young.
Es un milagro que se deje ver	It's so good to see you.

Dígame usted dónde se fue a meter.	Tell me, where have you been?

The importance of family as a core Hispanic/Latino value is represented in many of *Cri-Cri's* songs that tell about conversations with family members such as mother, father, and grandparents. One of these songs is called *Di por qué* (Say why) and it tells about the many questions a curious child asks *abuelita* (granny).

"Di por qué"	**"Say why"**
Di por qué,	Say why,
dime, abuelita,	say, Granny
di por qué	say why
eres viejita.	you are old.
Di por qué	Say why
sobre las camas	on the beds
ya no te gusta brincar	you don´t like to jump anymore.
Di por qué	Say why
usas los lentes,	you wear glasses,
y por qué	and why
no tienes dientes.	you don´t have any teeth.
Di por qué	Say why
son tus cabellos	your hair is like
como la espuma del mar	the foam of the sea.
Micifú	Micifú
siempre está	is always
junto al calor,	by the heater,

igual que tú.	just like you.
Di por qué	Say why
frente al ropero,	in front of the wardrobe
donde hay	where you have
tantos retratos,	so many pictures,
di por qué	say why
lloras a ratos,	you cry at times,
dime abuelita, por qué.	say granny, why.

In addition to telling stories, *Cri-Cri's* songs teach literacy through music. One song called *Marcha de las letras* (March of the letters) uses rhythm and rhyme to describe a parade where the vowels march.

"Marcha de las letras"	**"March of the letters"**
Que dejen toditos los libros abiertos	Leave all the books open
ha sido la orden que dio el general.	is the order the general gave.
Que todos los niños estén muy atentos,	Let all the children pay close attention
las cinco vocales van a desfilar.	the five vowels will now parade.
Primero verás	First you will see
que pasa la A	the A passing by
con sus dos patitas	with its two legs
muy abiertas al marchar	wide open while it marches.
Ahí viene la E	Here comes the E

alzando los pies.	raising its feet.
El palo de en medio	The stick in the middle
es más chico, como ves.	is shorter, as you can see.
Aquí está la I,	Here is the I
la sigue la O.	followed by the O.
Una as flaca y otra gorda,	One is skinny and the other one is fat,
porque ya comió.	because it already ate.
Y luego hasta atrás	And then at the back
llegó la U,	the U arrived,
como la cuerda	just like the rope
con que siempre saltas tú.	that you always use to jump.

In addition to *Cri-Cri*'s songs, *corridos* (Mexican epic songs) were fun to listen to. How I wished I could be one of the characters in *Cri-Cri* and *corridos* stories! The only way I could in fact make this happen was through theater-like play. Therefore, my sisters and I learned our favorite songs lyrics by heart, created scenarios in our grandmother's big patio, made costumes out of color tissue paper sheets and newspapers, and practiced, practiced, practiced! Our theater performances were often accompanied by samples of the original songs supplemented by dialogues we developed on our own. And if we were feeling even more creative, we used a simple tape recorder to create radio shows and record our stories along with our own special sound effects – just like in *Cri-Cri's* stories. When we felt ready to debut, we invited family members and friends to see us perform. There were many laughs, which were the best encouragement for our work-play.

Theater in the classroom. As a Bilingual and English as a Second Language methods instructor, I discuss with my students ways to incorporate multiple intelligences (Gardner, 1993) into our teaching, one of which is the design of theater-like stories that integrate the author's creativity and the use of technology. I often have my methods students select objectives from their K-12 curriculum and design lessons in groups, create and integrate their own stories or stories from songs they like, and come up with special sound effects as accompaniment. Many students integrate high-tech resources such as PowerPoint applications and digitized audio and video to their projects. With today's technology, possibilities are certainly endless!

Riddles

I grew up learning and making up riddles. I knew a round of riddles was about to start when I heard someone say: *"Adivina, adivinador..."* (Listen up, can you guess the following riddle(s)?). The following are some riddles I still know by heart today.

- *Boca arriba, vacío. Boca abajo, lleno.* (Upside down, I am empty. Otherwise, I am full. Who am I?).
  -- El sombrero. (A hat)
- *Adivina quién soy: Cuanto más lavo, más sucia voy.* (Guess who I am. The more I wash, the dirtier I get).
  -- El agua. (Water).
- *De celda en celda voy, pero presa no estoy.* (I go from cell to cell, but I am not in jail).
  -- La abeja. (A bee)

- *Sin salir de su casa, por todos sitios pasa.* (It goes everywhere without leaving home).
-- El caracol. (A snail).
- *¿Qué es lo que mientras más crece, más baja?* (The more they grow, the lower they go. What are they?).
-- Las raíces de los árboles. (Tree roots)
- *Ni lo puedes ver, ni vives sin él.* (You cannot see it, but you cannot live without it).
-- El aire. (Air).

Riddles are word games, usually presented in the form of questions and are dependent on phonological, morphological, lexical, or syntactic ambiguity (Pepicello & Weisberg, 1983). Riddles have been part of many cultures throughout history; the Greeks, Celts, Maya, and Aztecs all used this resource in their literature. Riddles or *adivinanzas* are part of the Hispanic oral tradition today – they are games where players (a) find the hidden meaning behind a phrase or statement or (b) provide solutions to enigmas expressed in brief statements. *Adivinanzas* are intrinsically motivating and elicit higher-order thinking and problem-solving skills (López-Díaz, 1998). In addition, skill in solving riddles is positively correlated with children's reading ability (Ely & McCabe, 1994) and the development of good reading comprehension skills (Yuil, 1998).

Riddles in the classroom. My approach to the use of riddles in the methods courses I teach today goes beyond having students learn and figure out popular riddles. Since many riddles in the Hispanic oral tradition use rhyme, I often have my students compose their own riddles and use rhyme, as well. Then, we share and evaluate the solutions we offer to the riddles we composed and compile our products in a classroom book. It is amazing what creative minds can achieve while they have fun exploring their oral traditions!

Teachers can also create a treasure chest of riddles, copying them onto index cards and placing the answers on the reverse of the cards. Then they can have students draw the answers or cut them out of old magazines and paste them. As an extension activity, students can be encouraged to create their own riddles about a specific topic they are studying or about the theme or characters of a book (Ada, 2003).

Dichos

My *abuelita* taught me most of the *dichos* I know. Grandma had twelve grandchildren, all of whom gathered at her house on Fridays. Every grandchild looked forward to *"viernes con mi abuelita"* (Fridays with grandma), especially because she let us draw imaginary houses with chalk on her patio, and because she cooked incredibly well. However, my *abuelita* had an unusual way of calling her grandchildren to the table and make sure we all came at once. She used to call out, *"Niños, ¡camarón que se duerme…!"* (Children, the careless shrimp….!). Yes, to call her grandchildren to the table, my grandmother used the beginning part of the well-known Hispanic *dicho* (or proverb) *"Camarón que se duerme, se lo lleva la corriente"* (The careless shrimp will be carried away by the current"). And we grandchildren knew exactly what she meant – she had twelve chairs at the dinner table, and twelve hungry grandchildren plus more than eight hungry adults. What my grandmother meant by *"Children, camarón que se duerme...!"* was "Children eat first, but if you do not come right this minute, an adult might take your chair and you will not be able to eat with your cousins." Once called we raced right to the dining table – this lesson we learned well and never forgot.

Dichos, proverbs, or sayings are based on irony, metaphors, and abstract concepts. They are spontaneous, brief, are stated with rhyme, and are transmitted orally from generation to generation. *Dichos* are cultural constructs that reflect people's beliefs and wisdom people turn to in times of need and tribulation (Zúñiga, 1992). They are widely used within the context of Hispanic Spanish speaking families' normal daily living. In addition, *dichos* are a means of transferring cultural values and beliefs to young generations on individual, family, and community levels by teaching and socializing children (Chahin, Villarruel, & Viramontes, 1999).

Dichos offer the advantages of allowing for cultural and familial relevance, vivid imagery (Aviera, 1996), high contextualization (Rogers, 1990), expression of individual creativity (Olinick, 1987), and are also a vehicle for the expression of attitudes (Winick, 1976). Moreover, *dichos* have been identified as tools that provide cultural contexts for discourse conducive to literacy development (López-Díaz, 1998). The following are some *dichos* my *abuelita* taught me that translate into similar proverbs or sayings in English:

- *Cuando el gato no está, los ratones se pasean.*
(When the cat's away, the mice will play).
- *Un lugar para cada cosa y cada cosa en su lugar.*
(A place for everything and everything in its place).

- *Donde una puerta se cierra, otra se abre.* (When one door shuts, another opens).
- *De tal palo, tal astilla.* (Literally, this means "like wooden stick, like splinter", but it translates into "Like father, like son.")
- *El que no oye consejo, no llega a viejo.* (Literally, this means "He who hears no advice will not get old," but it translates into "Advice when most needed is least heeded").

<u>Dichos</u> in the classroom.   Some classroom applications of *dichos* I have used in my practice as an ESL/EFL teacher include the following:

- *Script writing*: The class writes a dialogue by using only *dichos*. Conjunctions can be used, but only when necessary. These dialogues can become scripts the class will enact, or dialogues in cartoon strips the class creates.
- *Dicho matching*: The class writes *dichos* on separate slips of paper. They identify the *situation* and the *consequence or conclusion* in the *dichos*. Once these have been identified, the slips are cut in half leaving the situation apart from the consequence/conclusion. The class mixes all situations and all consequences in two different piles and then play by matching a situation with a consequence. The class can negotiate meaning among themselves and explain the reasons behind their decisions.
- *Dichos and morals*: The class uses stories they are reading, or stories they draw from their own experience. Stories similar in their structure to fables might lend themselves better to this kind of activity. The class can

share the stories with each other and then think of a *dicho* as a moral for their stories.

• *Framing stories*: This technique is very similar to the previous one, except here a volunteer starts with a *dicho* that frames a story not yet revealed to the rest of the class. After the "framing *dicho*" has been stated, the class will ask the volunteer questions to guess the characters and plot of the story framed by the *dicho*.

• *Dichos in other languages*: The class conducts research and finds out if there are *dichos* in other languages that convey a similar meaning to those in their first language.

Dichos provide appropriate cultural contexts for discourse conducive to literacy development, and therefore, they can be integrated in literacy programs. Along with a group of practitioners, I am currently developing an adult literacy program for Spanish speakers that uses *dichos* as its main theme. The program is culturally relevant and is designed for successful parental involvement programs in Texas.

Rondas and songs

I do not recall who taught me the lyrics to *rondas* and other children's songs that I know by heart. I only know I have known the tune and lyrics for as long as I can remember. Growing up with my cousins, friends, and other children at school, I often participated in *rondas* – songs in rhyme, meant to be sung by a group of children holding hands in a circle. One of my favorite *rondas* is called *Naranja Dulce* (Sweet Orange). The following is an excerpt from the *ronda*:

"Naranja Dulce"	**"Sweet orange"**
Naranja dulce,	Sweet orange,
limón partido,	sliced lime,
dame un abrazo	give me a hug
que yo te pido.	I ask of you.
Toca la marcha,	The march is playing,
mi pecho llora,	my heart is crying,
adiós señora,	good-bye my lady,
yo ya me voy	I am leaving now
a mi casita de sololoy	to my little house of *sololoy*
a comer tacos	to eat tacos
y no les doy.	and I will not share.

We used to sing *"Naranja Dulce"* while we held hands and turned in a circle. We took turns going to the middle of the circle and directing others as we sang and stopped briefly to act out the meaning of the underlined lines of the song (i.e., give me a hug, the march is playing, good-bye, etc.). When we became tired of repeating *Naranja Dulce* several times, we turned to other *rondas* like *El patio de mi casa* (The patio of my house), and *Arroz con leche* (Rice with milk).

"El patio de mi casa"	**"The patio of my house"**
El patio de mi casa	The patio of my house
es particular.	is singular.
Se lava y se plancha	It's washed and ironed

como los demás.	like others.
Agáchense	Bend everybody
y vuélvanse a agachar,	and bend again,
que todos los niños	all children
se saben agachar.	know how to bend.

"Arroz con leche"	**"Rice with milk"**
Arroz con leche,	Rice with milk.
me quiero casar	I want to marry
con una señorita	with a señorita
de la capital	from the capital
que sepa coser	who knows how to sew
que sepa border	who knows how to embroider
que sepa las tablas	who knows
de multiplicar .	the multiplication tables.
Con ésta, sí,	This one, yes,
con ésta, no,	this one, no,
con esta señorita	this señorita
me caso yo.	I will marry.

Participating in *rondas* was fun, especially because children of different ages joined, and all of us had an opportunity to teach younger siblings and friends how to sing and act out. An older sister, I witnessed how my younger siblings internalized the tunes and lyrics quickly – and how they managed to sing along (or so they thought), even when they could not yet pronounce appropriately many of the words they said. Little did I know years later I would call this native language acquisition and development. The rhymes in *rondas* and other children's songs consist of complex linguistic and narrative strategies that contribute to children's literacy development (Grugeon, 1999). In addition, the repetition of nursery rhymes, jingles and poems help children acquire phonemic awareness while encouraging play (Fisher & Williams, 2000).

Rondas in the classroom. I tell my students that *rondas* are excellent sources of culturally relevant instructional material that provide exposure to rhyme, sequencing, and coordination of motor skills, all of which are critical topics included in early childhood curricula. When *rondas* and other children's songs are carefully integrated to teaching, they can be powerful instructional tools that combine play while reinforcing language development. As a bilingual teacher, I often related circle songs or *rondas* to stories read in the classroom in order to extend and support the teaching of rhyme and sequencing for young children.

Trabalenguas

At home, we often challenged family and friends to say *trabalenguas* or tongue twisters as fast and accurately as possible. We started by timing how long it took players to say a *trabalenguas*, then those who were faster moved to the next level until only two competitors were left. One single hesitation and one of the players was out: We had a winner. To play, we usually started with the most common *trabalenguas* and then moved to less common ones. The following are some of my favorite tongue twisters:

- *Pepe Peña pela papa, pica piña, pita un pito, pica piña, pela papa, Pepe Peña.*
(Pepe Peña peals a potato, dices pineapple, blows a whistle, dices a pineapple, peals a potato.)
- *Compadre, cómpreme un coco. – No compadre, no compro coco, porque como poco coco como, poco coco compro.*
(*Compadre*, buy a coconut. – No, *compadre*, I won't buy a coconut, because since I eat very little coconut, I buy very little coconut.)
- *Cuando cuentes cuentos, cuenta cuantos cuentos cuentas, porque si no cuentas cuantos cuentos cuentas, nunca sabrás cuantos cuentos cuentas tú.*
(When you tell stories, count how many stories you tell, because if you don't count how many stories you tell, you'll never know how many stories you tell.)
- *Me han dicho que he dicho un dicho, mismo que no he dicho yo, porque si yo lo hubiera dicho, estaría muy bien dicho por haberlo dicho yo.*
(They have told me that I've said a saying, which I have not said, because if I had said it, it would have been well said, since I had said it.)
- *En el Este éste está. Está éste en el Este, pero el Este ¿en dónde está?*
(In the East this is. This is in the East, but where is the East?)

<u>Trabalenguas in the classroom.</u> *Trabalenguas* are difficult to say, but they help to practice articulation and pronunciation of words (López-Díaz, 1998). They are fun, and allow for

improvement of diction through play. As we discuss in my methods classes, *trabalenguas* can be great tools for fostering listening skills, for the practice and recognition of certain sounds, and for the teaching of reading, since they emphasize specific phonemes and syllable clusters. One should bear in mind, however, that tongue twisters should be treated with caution when used with second-language learners, for whom they can be very difficult. It is important that a spirit of joy and laughter accompany them and that no child be made uncomfortable for not being able to say them accurately (Ada, 2003).

Tap in

The Hispanic oral tradition is a wealth of resources that teachers can use for facilitating students' language acquisition and development. By incorporating elements of the Hispanic oral tradition in the classroom, not only do teachers make learning meaningful (Crawford , 1993; Fantini, 1991), but they also foster pride in the students' cultural identity (Ovando & Collier, 1998). Popular children's songs that allow for theater-like play, as well as riddles, *dichos*, *rondas*, and *trabalenguas* are available in our students' communities and represent a culturally and linguistically appropriate – albeit often untapped – resource for Spanish and English literacy development. It is up to our community, practitioners, and researchers to not only validate but *promote* the Hispanic oral tradition so that our children become living proof that *"Lo que bien se aprende, nunca se olvida."*

References

Ada, A. F. (2003). *A magical encounter: Latino children's literature in the classroom.* New York: Allyn and Bacon.

Aviera, A. (1996). "Dichos" therapy group: A therapeutic use of Spanish language proverbs with hospitalized Spanish-speaking psychiatric patients. *Cultural Diversity and Mental Health, 2*(2), 73-87.

Chahin, J., Villarruel, F. A., & Viramontes, R. A. (1999). Dichos y refranes: The transmission of cultural values and beliefs. In H. P. McAdoo (Ed.), *Family ethnicity: Strengthening diversity* (pp. 153-167). Thousand Oaks, CA: Sage.

Costigan, S., Muñoz, C., Porter, M., & Quintana, J. (1989). *El sabelotodo: The bilingual teacher's best friend.* Carmel, CA: Hampton-Brown Books.

Crawford, L. W. (1993). *Language and literacy: Learning in multicultural classrooms.* Needham Heights, MA: Allyn & Bacon.

De la Colina, J., Helguera L. I., García, A., García, A., García, F., Hinojosa, F., et al. (1999). *Francisco Gavilondo Soler Cri-Cri. Canciones Completas. Colección los trovadores. Vol. 1* Mexico: Ibcon.

Ely, R. & McCabe, A. (1994). The language play of kindergarten children. *First Language, 14,* 19-35.

Fantini, A. E. (1991). Bilingualism: Exploring language and culture. In L. M. Malavé & G. Duquette (Eds.), *Language, culture and cognition* (pp. 110-119). Clevedon, England: Multilingual Matters.

Fisher, R. & Williams, M. (2000). *Unlocking Literacy.* London: David Fulton.

Gardner, H. (1993). *Multiple intelligences: The theory in practice - A reader.* New York: Basic Books.

Grugeon, E. (1999). The state of playing: Children's oral culture, literacy and learning. *Reading, (33)*1, 13-16.

López-Díaz, G. (1998). Recursos a utilizar en la enseñanza de la lectura en Español. In A. Carrasquillo & P. Segan (Eds.), *The teaching of reading in Spanish to the bilingual student* (pp. 163-184). Mahwah, NJ: Lawrence Erlbaum Associates.

Olinick, S. L. (1987). On proverbs: Creativity, communication, and community. *Contemporary Psychoanalysis, 23*(3), 463-468.

Ovando, C. J. & Collier, V. P. (1998). *Bilingual and ESL classrooms. Teaching in multicultural classrooms.* New York: McGraw Hill.

Pepicello, W. J. & Weisberg, R. W. (1983). Linguistics and humor. In P. E. McGhee & J. H. Goldstein (Eds.), *Handbook of humor research.* New York: Springer-Verlag.

Rogers, T. B. (1990). Proverbs as psychological theories...or is it the other way around? *Canadian Psychology, 31*(3), 195-207.

Winick, C. (1976). The social contexts of humor. *Journal of Communication, 26*(3), 124-128.

Yuil, N. (1998). Reading and riddling: the role of appreciation in understanding and improving poor text comprehension in children. *Cahiers de Psychologie Cognitive/Current Psychology of Cognition, 17*(2), 313-342.

Zúñiga, M. E. (1992). Families and Latino roots. In E. W. Lynch & M. J. Hanson (Eds.), *Developing cross-cultural competence: A guide for working with young children and their families* (pp. 151-179). Baltimore: Paul H. Brookes Publishing.

Analyzing Some Persistent Errors in English Made by Vietnamese Speakers

Phap Dam
Texas Woman's University

Language educators distinguish two types of errors found in the interlanguages of language learners: developmental and interference. While developmental errors reflect a normal pattern of development common among all language learners, interference errors are caused by the learners' native languages. This paper deals with a number of persistent types of interference errors in English made by Vietnamese speakers, who were either former students of mine at the University of Saigon (1965-1975) or Vietnamese American writers whose articles I was asked to edit in the last 20 years or so. It should be noted that these students and writers were all learners of English as a foreign or second language. I will share my analysis of these particular errors and then make a recommendation on how to help Vietnamese speakers overcome these errors.

Some types of persistent errors in English made by Vietnamese speakers

It appears that these errors tend to occur when the syntactical structures of Vietnamese and English are strikingly different. In the scope of this paper, I will analyze the errors Vietnamese speakers persistently make in the following areas of English, which involve the handling of (1) linking verb "be" before adjectives, (2) indefinite and definite articles, (3) complicated verb tenses, (4) subject pronouns and object pronouns, and (5) complex sentences introduced by subordinate conjunctions.

Sentences containing errors are preceded by a pound sign (#), glosses of Vietnamese terms are kept inside square brackets ([ ]), and examples in both languages are inside quotation marks.

<u>(1) Linking verb</u>

The Vietnamese equivalent of the English linking verb "be" is "là." However, "là" is rarely used to link a subject with its predicative adjective in Vietnamese:

"Nó đói"

[He hungry]

"He is hungry."

"Giáo-sư Smith thông-minh vô cùng."

[Professor Smith intelligent without end]

"Professor Smith is extremely intelligent."

We may assume that Vietnamese adjectives have their own "built-in" verbs or that they function like "stative verbs." Errors reflecting this Vietnamese syntactic feature are found in the following:

"My child very sick today."

" Our elderly parents not happy to be away from Vietnam."

(2) Articles

Vietnamese learners of English know that English speakers sometimes use an indefinite article ("She is A funny girl" or "Charles was just AN average student"), sometimes a definite article ("That would be THE perfect solution to our problem"), and sometimes no article at all ("Dogs and cats are favorite pets in America"). Because A, AN, and THE have no exact counterparts in Vietnamese, Vietnamese learners of English are frequently at a loss to know which to use. This uncertainty causes them to write such flawed English sentences as:

" His dream is to become lawyer, not teacher."

" The exhausted man went to the bed without eating dinner."

" We truly hope that we will hear a good news soon."

(3) Verb tenses

When necessary, Vietnamese grammar can express time adequately by means of placing one of several aspect-marking particles in front of the main verb, notably "đã" (for past), "đang" (for present), and "sẽ" (for future):

"Hắn đã gặp một bạn cũ tuần rồi."

[He past-marker meet one friend old week just past]

"He met an old friend last week."

"Ông thầy đang dạy cú-pháp tiếng Việt."

[Mr. teacher present-marker teach syntax language Viet]

"The teacher is teaching Vietnamese syntax."

 "Khi có thì-giờ tôi sẽ thăm bác tôi tại Houston."

[When have time I future-marker visit father's older brother my in Houston]

"When I am free, I will visit my uncle in Houston."

With their native tongue lacking the intricate structure of tenses and moods found in English and other Western languages, Vietnamese speakers find English tenses other than present ("He IS at work today"), past ("Mary LOOKED so happy with her parents last week"), and future ("They WILL DO it for us this afternoon") hard to understand and use. Indeed, the handling of more complicated English tenses (especially those expressed by auxiliaries and past and present participles, like "We WILL HAVE BEEN LIVING in America for twenty years by then" and "If my parents HAD BEEN rich at that time, they WOULD HAVE SENT me to a private school in Switzerland") could qualify as the problem area in which they make the most errors. The serious mismatch in tense and mood systems between Vietnamese and English and the convenient simplicity of the Vietnamese system are the reason why Vietnamese learners of English keep writing such interference-induced sentences as:

"We live in California since 1975."

" I really wish I can speak English like you."

" If you are ten years younger, my brother will probably marry you."

It is worth noting that the above sentences reflect "correct" Vietnamese syntax, and that some Vietnamese learners of English deliberately avoid using complicated tenses in English, simply for fear of making mistakes.

(4) Subject pronouns and object pronouns

In English complex sentences, subordinate clauses, like main clauses, must have subjects and verbs. In a similar situation, however, the subordinate clause in Vietnamese usually <u>does not</u> require a subject:

"Cha tôi làm việc cho đến khi xỉu."

[Father my past-marker do work until faint]

"My father worked until he fainted."

"Nếu không có việc làm, họ sẽ không có đồ ăn."

[If no have jobs, they future-marker no have thing eat]

"If they do not have jobs, they will not have food."

Errors reflecting the above-mentioned tendency in Vietnamese syntax manifest themselves in the following:

" My father worked until fainted."

" If not have jobs, they will not have food."

In Vietnamese sentences, direct object pronouns are frequently "understood":

"Người đàn-ông ấy vô-lễ lắm nên không ai ưa."

[Person man that impolite very so nobody likes]

"That man is very impolite, so nobody likes him."

" Tặng bạn máy hình này. Tôi mua ở Nhật đấy!"

[Give friend machine picture this. I buy in Japan you know]

"This camera is for you. I bought it in Japan, you know."

Errors reflecting the above-mentioned tendency in Vietnamese syntax are found in the following:

"That man is very impolite, so nobody likes."

"This camera is for you. I bought in Japan, you know."

<u>(5) Complex sentences introduced by subordinate conjunctions</u>

English commonly begins a complex sentence with its subordinate clause led by a conjunction like "because," "although," "if," "even if," and so on. The main clause of the sentence then follows:

"Because he was reckless, he caused a terrible accident."

"Although my parents are poor, they are quite generous."

"If you did that thing, I would hate you."

"Even if she had time, she would not want to see you!"

When expressions of the type mentioned above are used in Vietnamese, it is usual for the main clause to be introduced by one of such "balancing words" as "nên," "thì," "nhưng," and "cũng." Transferring this deeply-ingrained syntactical habit into English causes errors:

"Vì nó cẩu-thả NÊN nó đã gây ra một tai-nạn khủng-khiếp."

[Because he reckless SO he past-marker cause an accident terrible]

"Because he was reckless, so he caused a terrible accident."

"Tuy song thân tôi nghèo NHƯNG ho khá hào-phóng."

[Although parents my poor BUT they quite generous]

"Although my parents are poor, but they are quite generous."

"Nếu anh làm chuyện đó THÌ tôi sẽ ghét anh."

[If you do matter that THEN I would hate you]

"If you did that thing, then I would hate you."

"Ngay cả nếu có thì-giờ nàng CŨNG không muốn thấy anh!"

[Even if have time she ALSO no want see you]

"Even if she had time, she also would not want to see you."

The reality of mother-tongue influence

The types of persistent interference errors made by Vietnamese speakers in English analyzed above do not appear to support the claim by some linguists that mother-tongue interference is negligible in interlanguage. This observation about undeniable mother-tongue influence is also shared by the authors of articles in a book covering 19 language backgrounds edited by Michael Swan and Bernard Smith (1987) entitled *Learner English.* It is a practical reference book which compares the relevant features of the students' own languages with English, helping teachers predict and understand the problems their students have. About the book's specialist contributors , Swan and Smith commented that:

> They are all clearly convinced that the interlanguages of the learners they are discussing are specific and distinct (so that it makes sense to talk about Thai English, Japanese English, Greek English and so on); and they all obviously see mother-tongue influence as accounting for many of the characteristic problems they described. (p. xi).

Expressing the same belief, Lily Wong Fillmore and Catherine Snow (2000) wrote in their paper entitled *What Teachers Need To Know About Language*:

> The native Chinese speaker who treats plurals and past tenses as optional rather than obligatory in English is reflecting the rules of Chinese. Of course such a learner needs to learn how to produce grammatical English sentences. But understanding the variety of structures that different languages and dialects use to show

meaning, including grammatical meaning such as plurality or past tense, can help teachers see the logic behind the errors of their students who are learning English. (p. 15).

It is now obvious that merely exposing learners to language is not enough and that a more form-focused approach is needed, because activities focusing on message alone are inadequate to help learners develop an accurate knowledge of the target language (Robinson, 1996; Dekeyser, 1998). I believe this form-focused approach is crucial when the structures of the target language and the learners' native one differ the most. In this situation, global "acquisition" activities are much less effective than analytic "learning" activities, which involve a conscious manipulation of language rules.

Intervention, sensitization, and consciousness-raising

Intervention by teachers is critical, as Fillmore and Snow (2000) cogently argued, "In order to teach effectively, teachers need to know which language problems will resolve themselves with time and which need attention and intervention" (p.7) in reaction to the fact that "over the past two decades, some teacher education programs and in-service workshops have suggested that there is no need to teach English directly" (p.24).

Sensitization (or using features of the learners' first language to help them understand the second) and consciousness-raising (or helping the learners by drawing attention to features of the second language) are effective ways for instructional intervention (Cook, 2001). Ever enthused about explicit grammar teaching, the author of *Second Language Learning And Language Teaching* confided:

The French subjunctive was explained to me at school not just to give me academic knowledge of the facts of French, but to help me to write French. After a period of absorption, this conscious rule was supposed to become part of my unconscious ability to use the language. (p. 41).

A five-step instructional intervention

Suppose you have noted that some of your Vietnamese-speaking students keep using the simple present tense instead of the present perfect tense to express an action that took place in the past but still continues at the moment of speaking (# "I am here since last week"), even though they have been exposed to the present perfect tense ("I have been here since last week") on numerous occasions. To help these students overcome this interference error in tense usage, you will do well by implementing the following five-step instructional intervention involving sensitization, consciousness-raising, practice, and rule-making:

Step 1

Lining up learners' output and standard counterpart:

(A) I am here since last week.

(B) I have been here since last week.

Step 2

Sensitization:

Inform the learners that sentence (A) reflects Vietnamese syntax, is a word-for-word translation from Vietnamese (Tôi ở đây từ tuần qua) into English, and therefore must be corrected.

Step 3

Consciousness-raising:

Ask students to look at sentence (B) and see how the verb form differs from that in sentence (A). Tell them that the verb "am" in sentence (A) is in the simple present tense, and that the verb "have been" in sentence (B) is in the present perfect tense. Remind them how the present perfect tense is formed (have / has + past participle of main verb) and used (to express an action that took place in the past but still continues at the moment of speaking).

Step 4

Practice:

Show learners additional sentences containing the present perfect tense, such as "John has been here since this morning" and "Our parents have lived in Texas for many years." Have them produce sentences of their own, using the present perfect tense correctly.

Step 5

Rule-making:

Help learners make a rule whereby they can form and use the present perfect tense in English, based on what they have consciously learned and successfully practiced. Check on their use of this tense periodically. Remember that old habits die hard!

References

Cook, V. (2001). *Second language learning and language teaching* (3rd ed.). London: Arnold.

Dam, P. (1980). *A contrastive approach for teaching English as a second language to Indochinese students.* San Antonio, TX: Intercultural Development Research Association.

Dam, P. (2001, February). *Old habits die hard: Persistent errors in English written by Vietnamese speakers.* Paper presented at the National Association for Bilingual Education, Phoenix, Arizona.

Dekeyser, R.M. (1998). Beyond focus on form: Cognitive perspective on learning and practical second language grammar. In C. Doughty & J. Williams (Eds.), *Focus on form in second language acquisition* (pp. 42-63). Cambridge, England: Cambridge University Press.

Fillmore, L. W., & Snow, C. E. (2000). *What teachers need to know about language.* Washington, DC: Center for Applied Linguistics.

Robinson, P. (1996). Learning simple and complex language rules under implicit, incidental, rule-search and instructed conditions. *Studies in Second Language Acquisition, 18,* 27-62.

Swan, M., & Smith, B. (Eds.). (1987). *Learner English.* Cambridge, England: Cambridge University Press.

A Symbiotic Relationship between Spanish and English

Luis A. Rosado
University of Texas at Arlington

Contacts with Spanish and English speakers in the United States have created a historical and linguistic connection between the two groups. This connection is symbiotic in nature because Spanish and English speakers have borrowed from each other's language to create new words and phrases to meet their communication needs. Spanish speakers have modified English words to comply with Spanish grammar, and have thus created new words. Conversely, English speakers have adapted Spanish words in such a way that often these cannot be recognized as loanwords from Spanish. The words and expressions created by these two language groups have been studied and treated with skepticism, and little has been said about the use of this information to support children learning both English and Spanish. This article provides an overview of the historical and linguistic association between the two languages, describes the results of this interaction, and presents suggestions as to how to use this information to promote metalinguistic awareness and enrich the lexicon of students in dual language settings.

Historical Overview

Spanish has been one of the most influential languages in the history of America and in the world. It is estimated that Spanish is spoken by over 350 million people in over 32 countries and regions of the world.[1] Spanish is the primary language of Spain, Mexico, Costa Rica, Nicaragua, Guatemala, El Salvador, Panama, the Canary Islands, Honduras, Puerto Rico, Cuba, Dominican Republic, Venezuela, Ecuador, Peru, Colombia, Argentina, Chile, Uruguay, Paraguay and Bolivia. Spanish is also spoken in lesser known places like Belize, the Philippines, Galápagos Islands, Gibraltar, parts of Morocco, the west coast of Africa, Equatorial Guinea, Andorra, and the United States (World Language Resources, n.d.; Gordon, 2005). A Spanish variety known as Ladino, spoken by descendants of Jews from Spain, is also used in Turkey and Israel (López, 2001). In the United States, Spanish is widely spoken by the estimated 35.6 million Latinos that live in the country (U.S. Census, 2000).

The Spaniards brought to America Castilian Spanish and other dialectal variations developed within Spain. Castilian was the official language of the kingdom of Castile. This language evolved from popular Latin after the Roman conquest of Hispania around the 3rd century A.D. (World Language Resources, n.d.). After the fall of the Roman Empire, Hispania was ruled by the Visigoths, and later by the Moors, an Arabic group from Northern

Africa.[2] The latter conquered most of Spain, and spent over seven centuries in power. As a result of this association, the Arabic language heavily influenced the Spanish language. In 1492 and under the leadership of the kingdom of Castile, the Moors were expelled from Spain. With the unification of Spain, Castilian became the dominant language of the country, and eventually the language of the Spanish Empire.

In the same year, Columbus claimed the new world for Spain and the colonization and dissemination of Spanish in America began. One of the most important dialectal variations brought to America was the Andalusian variety. This Spanish dialect has been identified as the foundation for the development of the Spanish spoken in the American continents (Dalby, 1998; Resnick, 1981). In America, Spanish became the *lingua franca* of the multiple linguistic groups living within the Spanish empire (Dalby, 1998). As a result of these linguistic contacts, a large number of words from Native American groups became part of Spanish. Some of the most influential linguistic groups were the Nahuatl of Mexico, the Incas from Peru, the Caribs and Tainos from the Caribbean, and the Araucan and Guarani from South America (Costigan, Muñoz, Porter, & Quintana, 1989). The linguistic influence of these groups together with the physical and cultural isolation of the new territories gave birth to new dialects of Spanish. These new dialectal variations became official languages in the multiple Spanish-speaking countries that emerged after the fall of the Spanish empire in America.

As a result of this disintegration, Mexico took control of a large portion of the Spanish empire, including the regions bordering the United States. The political and economic instability of Mexico and the growth of the United States resulted in political conflicts between the two countries and eventually in war. After the war between the two countries, a large portion of Mexico became part of the United States. This political change promoted linguistic contacts between Spanish and English speakers, creating a symbiotic relationship between the two languages.

A symbiotic relationship

The annexation of the American Southwest and later Puerto Rico in 1898 intensified contacts between speakers of Spanish and English. These contacts promoted the development of new language forms that combined elements from both languages. For instance, Spanish speakers took English words like *yard* and *roof* and through the application of Spanish grammatical and phonological patterns created new words like *la yarda* and *el rufo*. Contrary to popular belief, these new words are not linguistic aberrations developed randomly by uneducated people. Instead, these words have been created following linguistic intuition and grammar rules from both languages. At least three linguistic generalizations were used to modify the two words listed above: *la yarda* and *el rufo*.

1. Most English words end in consonants or consonant clusters, while in Spanish words end mostly in vowels.

2. Spanish nouns are either masculine or feminine, and gender is generally identified by articles and word endings.

3. Spanish requires gender agreement among articles, adjectives and nouns.

Based on these rules, Spanish speakers use a masculine article *el* and add an *o* at the end of the word "roof" to restate the gender and comply with gender agreement, thus creating the words *el* **rufo**. The word **la yarda** underwent a similar process. The addition of the final vowel *a* and the article *la* was used to comply with feminine gender agreement. Since Spanish grammar rules are used as a foundation for their creation, these words have been developed similarly and concurrently throughout the United States. Some of the most common grammar rules used to make these and other transformations follow.

Spanish rules used to modify English words
1. Formation of the infinitive. Regular Spanish verbs end in *ar*, *er*, and *ir*. The *ar* is the most common form, and it is the only structure used to make these transformations in English. That is, bilingual people generally do not use rules for the suffixes *er* or *ir* to adapt English words. For example, the English verbs *to pick* and *to check,* through the application of the *ar* rule, become *piquiar* and *chequear.*

2. Rules for the formation of the present participle ending in **ando** or **endo**. Regular Spanish verbs ending in *ar* use the suffix **ando** and those ending in *er* or *ir* take the **endo**. In the creation of the present participle for verbs borrowed from English, only the **ando** construction is used. Thus, the verb *cachar* ending with the suffix *ar* will have *cachando* as its present participle. In words like *cuitiar* (to quit) and *bloquiar* (to block), Spanish speakers add an *i* or an *e* before the *ar* to provide consistency to the transformation, but they follow the rule for the *ar* suffix to create the present participles *cuitiando* and *bloquiando.*

3. Using Spanish phonology to modify English words.

Spanish speakers modify or substitute the sounds of English to comply with Spanish phonology. When Spanish speakers find English sounds that are not present in Spanish, they either modify the sounds or replace them with the closest sound in Spanish. For example, Spanish does not have the following phonemes: the /z/ like in *zoo,* /ə/ like in *thank,* and the /v/ of vowel .[4] These kinds of substitutions can create semantic problems when English language learners (ELLs) pronounce words like *zoo* as *Sue, thank* as *tank* or *sank,* and *vowel* as *bowel.*

4. Word endings in Spanish and English. Most Spanish words end in vowels; thus, Spanish speakers add a vowel or vowels to English words ending in consonants or consonant clusters. Based on this feature, words like *gang* and *carpet* become *ganga* and *carpeta.*

5. Gender agreement in Spanish. Spanish requires agreement in gender and number, and agreement is usually marked with a morpheme at the end of the word. In the noun phrases *la hermosa niña* and *el hermoso niño,* the letters *a, e* and *o* in the article, adjective and noun provide the marking for feminine and masculine, respectively. Following this feature, Spanish speakers force gender agreement in English and create words like: *la troca* (the truck), and *el lonche* (the lunch).

6. Use of equivalent suffixes to create words. Spanish speakers use equivalent Spanish suffixes to modify English words. For example, the English morpheme *-er* linking a person with an occupation is often substituted with the Spanish equivalent *-ero.* Following this substitution, Spanish speakers modify the English word *trucker* or *roofer as troquero* and *rufero.*

7. Initial consonant clusters beginning with letter S. Spanish

does not have words with consonant clusters beginning with *S* in initial position like *sk, sm, sl, str...*; these clusters only occur in medial position in Spanish, and they are always preceded by the vowel *e* when occurring initially. Consequently, Spanish speakers will precede these clusters with an *e* to comply with Spanish rules when speaking English. This modification results in nonstandard pronunciation of words like *espeak, estring* and *esnow*.

8. Identifying a product by its brand name. For example, people have used the brand name *Xerox* as a generic name for photocopiers and even as a verb as in *to xerox a page*.

Table 1 presents additional examples of English words that have been morphologically or phonologically modified to comply with Spanish grammar, together with explanations of the rules used for the linguistic transformation.

Table 1.
Structural and Phonological Modifications of English Words

English words	Spanish Modification	Grammar Rules Involved
1. Cheating	1. Chitiando	Apply rule #1 and #2: Words ending in *ar* take the *ando* to create the present participle. This transformation creates the words listed in column two. The pronunciation of the word [*pushando*] as [*puchando*] is caused by the confusion between the *sh* (š) and *ch* (č) typical of Spanish speakers learning English.
2. Watching	2. Wachando	
3. Pushing	3. Pushando or Puchando	
4. Catching	4. Cachando	
5. Flirting	5. Flirtiando	

1. To pick 2. To quit 3. To check 4. To bluff 5. To punch	1. Piquiar 2. Cuitiar 3. Chequear 4. Blofear 5. Ponchar	Apply rule # 1: Using the ending of Spanish regular verbs to create the infinitive form.
1.Congressman 2.Two-base hit 3. Struck out	1.Cangrimán 2. Tubai 3. Estrucao	Apply rule #3: Phonological adaptation to comply with Spanish sound system. In Puerto Rico the word *cangrimán* makes allusion to the political power of a "US congressman," however, it is commonly used to describe an astute or perverse person (Pérez, n.d.).
1. Bunch 2. Junk 3. Lunch 4. Scratch 5. Strike-out	1. Bunche 2. Junke 3. Lonche 4. Escrachar 5. Estrucar	Apply rule #5 to comply with gender agreement in words like *lonche* and *junke*. Most Spanish words ending in *e* are masculine. Apply rule # 7 to precede the clusters with S in the words *escrachar* and *estrucar*.
1. Wash 2. Dance	1. Washateria 2. Danceteria	Apply rule # 1 to create the word *washar*, and rule #6 to change the word from a verb to a noun as in *washateria* and *danceteria*. The Spanish suffix *-teria* refers to a place where

		something is manufactured or done.
1. Blender 2. Crayon 3. Diapers 4. Game con- sole 5. Copier	1. Osterizer 2. Crayola 3. Pampers 4. Nintendo 5. Xerox	Apply rule #8 to use the name brand as the name of the product.
1. Truck 2. Boss	1. La troca 2. La bosa	Apply rule # 4 and #5 to end the word in a vowel and to add the feminine marking of the word *la troca*. In this particular case the truck becomes feminine for the connection with the word *camioneta* used in Mexican Spanish. *La bosa* (the boss) is used to add the feminine marking.
1. Truck**er** 2. Rock**er** 3. Roof**er**	1. Troqu**ero** 2. Roqu**ero** 3. Ruf**ero**	Apply rule # 4 and #6 to replace the English suffix *-er* with the equivalent Spanish suffix *-ero*. It also identifies the word as masculine by using the *o* at the end of the word. For a female trucker, the word is *troquera*.

Adaptation of Spanish words

English speakers have also used similar linguistic creativity, and language borrowing to enrich and meet their communication needs (Rosado & Salazar, 2003). Based on this need, English speakers adopted Spanish words, and adapted them to comply with English phonology. Some of these words are part of the Southwest regional dialects while others have become part of the English spoken in the nation in general.

Loanwords from Spanish[3]

In the American Southwest, most words related to geography, ranching and agriculture are Mexican or Spanish in origin. Some of these words became English-Spanish cognates, while others have been structurally and phonologically modified in such a way that native Spanish speakers might not recognize their origin (Rosado & Salazar, 2003). Table 2 presents examples of these words.

Table 2
Spanish Words Structurally and Phonologically Adapted

Spanish Word	English Word	Meaning/ Explanations
Alameda	Almeda	A walkway surrounded by alamo trees (poplars)
Atún	Tuna	The fish
Banco or banca	Bunco	A bank or a person holding the money
Bandolera	Bandolier	Belt used across the shoulders by outlaws (bandoleros)
Bobo	Boob	Silly, naive person
Bosque	Bosky	Shady, woody
Cabaña	Cabana	A cabin

Calabozo	Calaboose	A prison cell or dungeon
Calentura	Calenture	Fever
Cañón	Canyon	Geography term
Chaparreras	Chaps	Leather trousers used by a cowhand
Cinchar	To cinch	To saddle a horse
Cucaracha	Cockroach	The insect
Desesperado	Desperado	Phonological adaptation of the word desperate
El lagarto	Alligator	An amphibian
Estacada	Stockade	A tall fence constructed of long stakes
Estibador	Stevedore	A person that loads a ship or container
Juzgado	Hoosegow	Jail
La riata or reata	Lariat	A rope used to round up livestock
Mesteño	Mustang	Unbranded horse
Vaquero	Buckaroo	Cowhand

In addition to words that have been considerably modified, English has also incorporated words with similar spelling. These words were probably learned orally and then through phonetic spelling incorporated into English. Table 3 contains a list of these words.

Table 3

Spanish Words with Similar Spelling

Spanish	English	Meaning/Explanations
Anchova	Anchovy	A small fish
Barricada	Barricade	Street barrier
Cacao	Cocoa	Chocolate beans
Caramelo	Caramel	A syrup made of burned sugar or a candy
Estampida	Stampede	Out of control cattle
Filibustero	Filibuster	The use of obstructive tactics by a member of the legislature
Galeón	Galleon	A large Spanish ship
Galón	Gallon	The liquid measure or the adornment used in hats
Granada	Grenade	The explosive
Guitarra	Guitar	The musical instrument
Jabalina	Javelina	Female wild boar
Lazo	Lasso	A loop on a rope
Mulato or mulata	Mulatto	The offspring of black and white parents
Ocelote	Ocelot	A wild cat
Picaresco	Picaresque	From the word picaroon, mischievous
Plátano	Plantain	Fruit larger than the banana used for cooking
Renegado	Renegade	Traitor or deserter
Sabana	Savannah	Grassland

Sarape	Serape	Heavy shawl worn over the shoulders
Tabaco; Cigarro	Tobacco; cigar	The plant and the product of tobacco
Tomate	Tomato	From the Nahuatl *tomatl*
Vainilla	Vanilla	A flavoring

English has also adopted words with the same spelling, but these are pronounced with the English intonation following English phonology. Accent marks and sometimes the tildes have been eliminated from the English version of the words. Table 4 contains a list of these words.

Table 4
Spanish and English Words with Identical Spellings

Spanish Word	Definition or comments
Adios	Good bye
Adobe	Clay used to build houses
Alfalfa	Food for cattle
Arena	It refers to the sports arena only, not the sand
Armada	In reference to the Spanish ships
Barracuda	The fish
Barrio	Latino neighborhood
Bonanza	Calm or quiet place, or rich ore shoot
Bongo	The musical instrument
Bronco, pinto and palomino	Terms for horses. Palomino refers to a white dove

Cafe and cafeteria	Coffee or a place to have a meal
Caliche	A hard soil typical of semiarid regions
Cantina, piñata, fiesta, tequila	Elements linked to entertainment
Cargo	Materials or merchandise to be transported
Corral, rodeo	A ring or fenced arena where animals may be separated or shown
Chaparral	A bird , the roadrunner (chaparral cock)
Chocolate	From the Nahuatl *xocolatl*
Compadre and comadre	Godfather and godmother, or a friend
Conquistador	Spanish conqueror
El Niño	Weather phenomenon; literally, it means the boy (Jesus)
Fandango	A sensuous and lively Spanish dance or a fight
Guacamole	Avocado dip
Guerrilla	Guerrilla warfare
Hacienda, hacendado	A large plantation, the owner of the *hacienda*
Incomunicado	Isolated
Jalapeño, habañero, and cilantro	Peppers and spices
Lobo, burro, armadillo	Animals of the American Southwest
Machete	The cutting tool, derived from the

	word *macho*
Mañana	Tomorrow, may imply procrastination
Mariachi	A Mexican band composed typically of itinerant street musicians
Marijuana or marihuana	An illegal controlled substance
Matador	Bull fighter
Mesa	Flat- topped elevation
Mestizo	A person of mixed race
Padre	Catholic priest
Patio	Courtyard
Patrón	The boss or foreman
Peón	Unskilled worker
Plaza	A public square in a city
Presidio	A military post, or the name of a city in Texas.
Pronto	Hurry up!
Remuda	A group of fresh horses
Salsa	Sauce or the Caribbean music
Sangria	An iced drink based on fruits, red wine and fruit juice
Sierra	Mountain range
Silo	A place to store grain or nuclear weapons
Sombrero	Hat, derived from the word *sombra* (shadow)
Taco, burrito, tortilla, nachos	Foods of Mexican or Mexican-American origin

Vigilante	A person who takes the law into his own hands

Linguistic groups from Central America, the Caribbean, South America, and the Moors contributed numerous words to Spanish. Through Spanish, these words have been added to English. Table 5 contains a list of such words.

Table 5
Selected Linguistic Contributions from Other Languages

Carib and Taino	Quechua, Araucanian, and Guarani	Arabic
Mosquito, peccary, manatee, cayman, canoe, cannibal, yucca , hammock, barbecue, hurricane, rumba, cha-cha, maize, maguey, guava, bongo, papaya.	Condor, llama, alpaca, vicuña, jaguar, jerky, charqui, coca, cocaine, potato, guano, quinella, pampas, gaucho, poncho.	Albatross, gazelle, mosque, jasmine, sugar, alcohol, acequia, admiral, algebra, syrup, talisman, tariff, zero, alkali, arsenal, carat, Koran, elixir, lemon, monsoon, safari, saffron, sofa, alcove.

Spanish expressions used in English

English has also adopted and popularized Spanish words and expressions including some whose connections to Spanish have been lost. For example the noun *ten-gallon hat* refers to a cowboy hat in Texas. People get confused with this name because they associate the word gallon with the liquid measure, while in reality the term *galón* in Spanish has an alternate meaning. It is the number of braids that circled the hat in place of a hatband, or the shoulder marking used to show military rank. Thus, the ten-gallon hat does not refer to the liquid measure or the size of the hat but the adornment used on it (Clark, 1996).

The expression *Give me the whole enchilada* makes allusion to the multiple ingredients used to make the Mexican dish. People don't know what is in there, but they want everything on it, the whole enchilada. The expression *mano a mano* makes reference to a fight without weapons or hand-to-hand combat. The expression *no más* or no more, makes allusion to the boxing match between Roberto "mano de Piedra" Durán and Sugar Ray Leonard. Currently, the expression *no más, no más* is used to imply giving up. As contacts with Spanish speakers increase, additional words and expressions will be added to English.

The influence of Spanish has also infiltrated the entertainment industry. As early as the 1950s, Speedy González, a stereotypical representation of Mexican character, introduced to the American public Spanish expressions like *¡Andale, ándale, arriba, arriba!* Desi Arnaz, in the popular show *I Love Lucy*, charmed the American audience with his strong Cuban Spanish accent and the occasional use of Spanish words and monologues. More recently, Arnold Schwarzenegger popularized the expression *Hasta la vista baby* in the movie *The Terminator*. Ricky Martin introduced the expression *live the crazy life* to the American public with his hit *Livin' la Vida Loca*. The expression *¿comprende, no comprende?* has been used in multiple movies and television shows, and now people use it for emphasis in conversations. Bart Simpson from the television show *The Simpsons* popularized the expression *¡Ay caramba!* Most people might not understand the meaning of these expressions, but they understand the context and use them accordingly. Spanish words and expressions are becoming a household element in the United States. With the continued influx of Latino immigrants and the natural growth of U.S.-born Spanish speaking groups, this influence will continue enriching the lexicon of American English.

Recommendations for teachers in dual language settings

Teachers in dual language programs need to use the linguistic knowledge that children bring to the learning process as a foundation for future learning. Spanish heritage speakers might bring to school a hybrid type of language that combines Spanish and English features. Native English speakers in Texas, on the other hand, might bring an English variety which has been enhanced and enriched through contacts with Spanish speakers. Teachers in dual language settings must seize this opportunity and explore the implicit linguistic knowledge that both groups bring to school. Some of the recommendations to take advantage of the linguistic connection between Spanish and English follow.

- Analyze the rules that Spanish speakers use to create new words in English and guide them to compare these new words with standard equivalent standard words in Spanish and English.
- Discuss with students how English speakers have adapted Spanish to create new English words and

expressions. Guide them to acknowledge and value the contribution of Spanish to the development of English.

• Accept the natural language that children bring to the classroom, but methodically, through implicit and explicit instruction guide them to use the standard forms of each language.

• Guide children to establish language boundaries to develop mastery in both languages. Language separation constitutes one of the main principles in successful dual language programs.

• Introduce English/Spanish cognates and deceptive cognates, and guide students to use the connection between the two languages to enrich the lexicon in both languages.

• Discuss with students the concepts of standard and nonstandard forms of both languages in a comparative fashion, and guide them to use each variety in the appropriate contexts to achieve the goal of becoming bilingual and bidialectal.

Conclusions

The historical association between Spanish and English has created a strong connection between the two languages. Spanish speakers have combined English and Spanish to create new words and expressions, and English speakers have done the same with Spanish, adding new words to the English lexicon. In the past, this connection was virtually ignored and construed as corruptions of the languages. However, with the new emphasis on two-way dual language instruction in Texas and the nation (Rosado, 2005), teachers should reexamine the connection between the two languages and use this information as a foundation to promote the meta-linguistic awareness that children need to achieve one of the main goals of dual language programs which is to help students become truly bilingual.

References

Ayto, J. (1990). *Dictionary of word origin: The history of more than 8,000 English-language words.* New York: Arcade Publishing.

Campbell, G. (1998). *Compendium of the world's languages* (Vol. 2). New York: Routledge Publishing.

Clark, T. L. (1996). *Western lore and language: A dictionary for enthusiasts of the American west.* Salt Lake City: University of Utah Press.

Costigan, S., Muñoz, C., Porter, M., & Quintana, J. (1989). *El sabelotodo: The bilingual　　teacher's best friend.* Carmel, CA: Hampton-Brown Books.

Dalby, A. (1998). *Dictionary of languages: The definite reference to more than 400 languages.* New York: Columbia University Press.

Del Toro y Gisbert, M. (1970). *Pequeño Larousse ilustrado* (7th ed.). Nápoles, México: Editorial Larousse.

Global Reach (n.d.). *Global Internet Statistics.* Retrieved October 10, 2005, from http://www.glreach.com/globstats/index.php3

Gordon, R. G., Jr. (Ed.). (2005). Languages of the world. [Electronic version]. *Ethnologue: Languages of the World* (15th ed.). Dallas: SIL International.

López, L. (2001). *Spanish: Facts about the world's languages: An encyclopedia of the world major languages, past and present.* New York: The H.W. Wilson Company.

Pérez, L. N. (n.d.). *Cangrimanes y Pañamanes*. Retrieved October
    21, 2005, from RedBetances.com Web site:
    http://www.redbetances.com/html/espanol/Cangrimanes%20y
    %20panamanes.htm
Resnick, M. C. (1981). *Introducción a la historia de la lengua
    española*. Washington, DC: Georgetown University Press.
Rosado, L., & Salazar, D. (2003). "La conexión: The English/
    Spanish connection." *National Forum of Applied
    Educational Research Journal 15 (4)*, 51-66.
Rosado, L. (2005, Spring). The state of Texas: Breaking new
    ground in dual language instruction. *TABE Journal, 8(1)*, 13-23.
Santamaría, F. (2000). *Diccionario de mejicanismos*. (6th ed.).
    Mexico, DC: Editorial Porrúa,S.A.
U.S. Census (2000). *The Hispanic population: Census 2000 brief.*
    U.S. Department of Commerce, Economics and Statistics
    Administration. Retrieved September 20, 2005, from
    http://www.census.gov/prod/2001pubs/c2kbr01-3.pdf
Ulibarri, S. R. (1991). *Kissing cousins: 1,000 words common to
    English and Spanish*. Albuquerque, NM: Fog Publications.
World Language Resources (n.d.). *Spanish language*. Retrieved
    October 20, 2005, from
    www.worldlanguage.com/languages/Spanish.html?calledfrom=5002

Footnotes

[1] To compare estimates of the number of Spanish speakers in the world,
    see Global Reach (n.d.), López (2001), and Gordon (2005).
[2] For a brief history of the Spanish language, see Campbell (1998), and
    López (2001).
[3] For additional information about these and other loanwords from
    Spanish see Santamaría (2000), Clark (1996), Ayto (1990), Ulibarri
    (1991), and Del Toro y Gisbert (1970).
[4] The difference between the phoneme /v/ and /b/ is taught in Puerto
    Rican Spanish. However, in daily speech, speakers of Puerto Rican
    Spanish have the tendency to suppress the /v/ sound.

Dichos and Proverbs as Culturally Relevant Literature

Mary Garza
Texas Woman's University

Introduction

Thomas and Collier (1997) proposed a conceptual model of how language acquisition occurs in bilingual school settings. Known as the Prism Model, it consists of four major components that are interrelated and interdependent. At the center of the structure are the social and cultural processes, with academic development, language development, and cognitive development in the native language and the target language forming the three sides of the prism. In light of this vital interrelationship and interdependence, bilingual teachers look for bridges to connect two languages and cultures. It is the purpose of this paper to show that English proverbs and Spanish *dichos*, when used effectively in the bilingual classroom, can create a socio-cultural bridge that demonstrates how separate cultures are similar to each other in both thought and language.

Dougall (2006), arguing in favor of using *dichos*, maintains that proverbs provide "an authentic insider's view of a culture" and that they "provide a snapshot of other cultures that allows for a more thorough understanding of both language and culture" (p. 1).

Dougall offers several reasons for using proverbs as a vehicle for language acquisition, including the following:

- Each saying provides "a mental picture that is readily comprehensible to educated readers of both Spanish and English."

- Insights gleaned from the study of proverbs will help students to better understand their own language and culture when analyzed comparatively.

- Proverbs help us understand diverse viewpoints.

Using proverbs and *dichos* in the bilingual classroom can provide a language and culture bridge from the home culture to English without losing relevance for the first language. According to Thomas and Collier (1997), the use of culturally relevant materials makes for easier transfer from one culture to another. The following listing of proverbs is intended for teachers' use in the classroom.

Categories of *dichos, refranes,* sayings or proverbs—Spanish to English

Authentic proverbs in Spanish below appear in italics while equivalent English proverbs are not italicized. Advice/caution/ warnings, behavior, nature and animals, and miscellany are the categories that have been selected.

Advice/Caution/Warning

1. *No dejes para mañana lo que puedas hacer hoy.*
   Don't put off for tomorrow what you can do today.

2. *El que ama al peligro, perecerá en él.*
   If you live by the sword, you will die by the sword.

3. *Dime con quien andas, y te diré quien eres.*
   Birds of a feather flock together.

4. *En la unión está la fuerza.*

In unity there is strength.

5. *No hay mal que por bien no venga.*
Every cloud has its silver lining.

Behavior

1. *Al que madruga, Dios le ayuda.*
The early bird gets the worm.

2. *Quien bien su obra empieza, la mitad tiene hecha.*
Beginning is half the work.

3. *Hoy para tí y mañana para mí.*
Scratch my back, and I'll scratch yours.

4. *Quien anda con sabios, sabio será; y quien con burros, rebuznará.*
You are known by the company you keep.

5. *Perro que ladra no muerde.*
His bark is worse than his bite.

Nature and animals

1. *Una golondrina no hace el verano.*
One swallow does not a summer make.

2. *Más vale pájaro en mano que cien volando.*
A bird in the hand is worth two in the bush.

3. *A caballo regalado no se le mira el diente.*
Don't look a gift horse in the mouth.

4. *Mente sana en cuerpo sano.*
Healthy mind, healthy body.

5. *En boca cerrada, no entran las moscas.*
Loose lips sink ships.

Miscellaneous

1. *No todo lo que brilla es oro.*
Not all that glitters is gold.

2. *Un lugar para cada cosa y cada cosa en su lugar.*
   A place for everything and everything in its place.

3. *Más vale maña que fuerza.*
   The pen is mightier than the sword.

4. *Aunque la mona se vista de seda, mona se queda.*
   You can't make a silk purse out of a sow's ear.

5. *La experiencia es la madre de ciencia.*
   Necessity is the mother of invention.

Implications for the classroom

There are several good reasons for using proverbs in classrooms. First, proverbs are a rich source for culture and language development. They can serve to expand discussion, vocabulary and understandings about the history and culture of people. Second, they provide an arena for discussion of life and how it is perceived by different groups of people—one's own and others. Third, they can show similarities of cultures when exploring similar or parallel ways of life. And fourth, the study of proverbs and *dichos* can enlist the help of parents, grandparents, aunts and uncles, and even community members in significant ways. In summary, proverbs and *dichos* are a rich source of history, culture, and commentary about life. The following are some specific and effective ways that teachers can use these sayings in English and Spanish in the classroom.

Suggestions for classroom use

While the suggestions below apply primarily to the elementary bilingual classroom, students and teachers in the upper grades may benefit from them as well.

- As an introduction or concluding activity, teachers may include proverbs and *dichos* posted around the room for students to read and memorize.
- Teachers might choose to have an individual proverb written on the board for penmanship practice as students enter the classroom to get ready for the day.
- In a writing center, proverbs written on cards or sentence strips can be placed where students practice writing them from models.   Students may want to write a story incorporating proverbs and *dichos*.   The stories can be made into classroom books and put in the reading center.   Students may also draw pictures of the literal meaning of a proverb or *dicho* and write a brief explanation of their illustration.
- In the listening center, students can listen to tape recordings of sayings and their translations.   If students write stories incorporating proverbs, these can be recorded and placed in the listening center.
- Older students may want to search the Internet for websites that include lists of proverbs in Spanish and English. They may then make a list of comparisons between the proverbs and their equivalents found on each list.
- Other uses may include posting and reading a proverb during calendar time as a *"Dicho del día."*
- The simplest and most literal sayings usually work best for the early grades, 1-3.   For example, a great saying for first graders is the following: *En boca cerrada no entran las mosca.* The teacher can lead the class, through discussion, to discover that on some occasions it could be best to keep one's mouth closed.   First graders can brainstorm about occasions where it

might be necessary to talk, while other occasions might be best for remaining silent, as teachers review or revise the rules of the room.

- Teachers can also pick sayings for first graders that are easy to visualize. *Al mejor mono le cae el zapote*, even the best monkey will drop the fruit, is pretty humorous in the eyes of first graders.

- In contrast to the kindergarten and first grade crowd, fifth graders will be able to handle sarcasm and deeper underlying meanings. *Aunque la mona se vista de seda, mona se queda* is an example for this type of analysis.

- Students can interview their parents or even grandparents to examine the forms or variants of statements such as *Perro que ladra no muerde* and *Perro ladrador, poco mordedor.*

- Fifth graders can interview their community or extended family members to see if they can document additional sayings.

- *Dime con quien andas y te diré quien eres* could lead to a discussion about being careful as to whom you associate with.

- Bilingual dictionaries can be useful for finding appropriate proverbs and *dichos.*

Conclusion

Proverbs and *dichos* have the potential to provide rich discussions, ponderings, and new insights through a literacy approach. They enrich the available resources a teacher may use when implementing a program of culturally relevant teaching. The study of proverbs and *dichos* can provide a two-way bridge for learning about the universality of human cultures everywhere and may contribute to a welcoming and accepting classroom environment for all students.

References

Castillo, C., & Bond, O.(1977). *University of Chicago Spanish dictionary* (3rd ed.). Chicago: The University of Chicago Press.

Dougall, D. M. (2006). *Why learn proverbs?* Retrieved March 16, 2006 from http:www.proverbios.com/articulos/art0.htm.

Ovando, C. J., Combs, M. C., & Collier, V.P. (2006). *Bilingual and ESL classrooms: Teaching in multicultural contexts* (4th ed.). Boston: McGraw Hill.

Spanish proverbs with translations –Spanish language: Proverbial Spanish, part 2: Translations. Retrieved March 16, 2006 from http://spanish.about.com/library/weekly/aa031901b.htm#5.

Thomas, C. J. & Collier, V. P. (1997). *School effectiveness for language minority students.* Washington, DC: National Clearinghouse for Bilingual Education.

Substance, Sense, and Sensitivity: A Veteran Bilingual Educator's Thoughts on Curriculum

Rita Deyoe-Chiullan
Richland College and Southern Methodist University

Regarding positive curriculum development models

There are some valuable movements among professional educators that have the potential to re-focus curriculum and instruction to meet the complex and varied needs of our increasingly diverse student population while simultaneously seeking to make the content learned more substantial, cognitively complete, relevant and challenging. Of signal importance is the just published monograph *Integrating Differentiated Instruction and Understanding by Design* (Tomlinson & McTighe, 2006) which marries the thorough restructuring of the curriculum proposed by Wiggins and McTighe in the *Understanding by Design* (2005) construct they have been developing over a number of years with a similarly extensive effort by Tomlinson in her work with differentiated instruction. An effort to harness the power of teaching with technology in tandem with the powerful concepts of profound and significant meaningful outcomes which respond to "essential questions" is evident in the valuable materials provided by the Intel Teach to the Future project. I have found that working with these innovative structures and conceptually rich ideas has given the experienced bilingual teachers in my graduate courses renewed encouragement to teach beyond the test.

At the same time, the consciousness of increasing demands to level the playing field so that all learners can experience success is clearly attested by resources such as efforts by Richard LaVoie and Mel Levine, whose work is made easily accessible to both novice and experienced teachers in multimedia VHS and/or DVD formats with titles such as *Beyond F.A.T. City* (LaVoie, 2005a) and *Learning Disabilities and Social Skills—Last One Picked, First One Picked On* (LaVoie, 2005b) and *MisUnderstood Minds* (Kirk, 2004).

The February 2006 issue of *Educational Leadership* contains fourteen major articles on varied aspects of the theme "Helping Struggling Students" and includes issues of race, gender, ethnicity, language and disabilities. These articles demonstrate the need to *"Teach Me Different!"* (American University, 2001) which was very well illustrated in the series of four videos bearing that title, featuring the Sally L. Smith methodology for learning-disabled students.

Other concerns experienced and expressed by parents and teachers relate to increased needs for schools to provide discipline and behavioral guidance to both students and their parents. This is evidenced by the rapid growth in popularity of materials produced by the Love and Logic Institute (Fay & Funk, 1995). All kinds of students have a great need to learn to solve the problems of everyday life by making good decisions in a healthy and appropriate manner (Funk, 2002) and, increasingly, parents of all ethnicities need support (Cline & Fay, 1990) in learning how to parent the "millennium student," just as teachers need guidance in modifying their approaches and attitudes when confronted by the changing expectations of their pupils (Nasseh, 1996).

Specific new curriculum materials of interest to teachers of ELLs

I regard it as a positive advance when I encounter new materials and initiatives that are supported by the teachers who are using them or that I feel would have enabled me to be a more effective classroom teacher at the elementary and secondary school level.

I am impressed by the potential offered by *Keys to Learning: Skills and Strategies for Newcomers* (Chamot, Keatley, & Anstrom, 2005). It is a much needed, carefully researched and developed resource for newcomer ELLs who arrive in the upper grades with limited previous academic access. Although not explicitly intended for such populations, it is also a good resource for learners whose English language learning is limited due to learning problems that are within the areas served by special education programs. The companion *Shining Star* 5-level program (Chamot, Huizenga, & Hartmann, 2005) for ELLs grades 6-12 that further develops literacy and sheltered content for these learners is also promising, as are the Longman content area texts, also for ELLs in grades 6-12. In particular, as I compared *Longman Science* (Pearson Education, 2006) to materials from other sources for ELLs in this age group, it was the only one with coherent, meaningful content that was well developed and fully understandable. Most of the others I looked at contained bits and pieces of diluted content information in formats that would be insulting and belittling to the upper grades student.

For younger learners (reading levels grades 3-6), I am particularly delighted with the engaging and beautifully prepared supplemental reading materials with extensive multicultural and cross-curricular social studies, language arts, science and math content in the *WorldScapes/Vistas del mundo* leveled literacy resource published by ETA Cuisenaire (2005). It is an impressive endorsement that when I sent a sample copy of these materials home with one of my undergraduate students for her to complete a materials evaluation assignment, she was unable to return it promptly because her nine-year-old son was unwilling to part with the book until he had finished reading it!

I have yet to encounter the resource I would want to put in the hands of every bilingual teacher who teaches children to read in Spanish although I have seen a few scholarly articles that I ask students to read as we discuss teaching strategies and appropriate interventions (Alanis, Munter, & Tinajero, 2003; Alanis & Tinajero, 2004). For any teacher who teaches children to read in English I would certainly wish they could own or have the use of Miriam Trehearne's *Comprehensive Literacy Resource for Grades 1-2 Teachers*, published by ETA Cuisenaire (2005). This is probably the one book I feel would have helped me the most as a classroom teacher to organize my literacy curriculum and instruction more confidently and effectively. Each of these *Comprehensive Literacy Resource* compendia is a wonderful resource for the grade level(s) addressed. However, the book for Grades 1-2 is the one that would either guide a new teacher to teach literacy successfully with few other resources in circumstances where teachers lack materials or to make appropriate selections in a school where shelves full of potential resources crowd and shout for attention, leaving the novice teacher in danger of sampling all and utilizing none.

Delightful, meaningful, authentic curriculum resources cannot overcome some of the errors in our current implementation of learning programs for English Language Learners, but thoughtful use of them and positive advocacy can certainly make the struggle to meet our challenges seem less tedious and more rewarding. Certainly, there are wonderful opportunities to increase the success of all our ELLs and their peers if new and veteran teachers continue to seek to understand and implement the best of the new materials in the context of the best new models for curriculum and instruction. We should focus on

- Materials which exhibit serious attention to *substance, sense* and *sensitivity* with authentic academic language in a coherent cultural context in every language in which learning and instruction occur.

- Curriculum constructs such as *Understanding by Design* (Wiggins & McTighe, 2005), which aim to develop a deeper, more relevant and meaningful context for learning by working back from worthwhile learning outcomes to the essential questions that will be answered by completing the learning tasks.

- Instructional imperatives such as differentiated instruction within a context of challenging all students to achieve (Tomlinson & McTighe, 2006).

- Consideration of the needs of children and parents for the support of schools to help us face, enjoy and reconstruct our amazing world of technology and globalization (Fay & Funk, 1995; Funk, 2002; Cline & Fay, 1990; Nasseh, 1996).

References

Alanis, I., Munter, J., & Tinajero, J. V. (2003). Preventing reading failure for English language learners: Interventions for struggling first-grade L2 students. *NABE Journal of Research and Practice 1*(1), 92-109.

Alanis, I., & Tinajero, J. V. (2004). *Preventing reading failure for English language learners: Interventions for struggling first grade L2 students.* TWU Reading Recovery and Early Literacy Conference, November 17-18, 2004, Dallas, Texas. Retrieved March 16, 2006 from http://www.dmc.utep.edu/bhgiza/pdf/alaniz_tinajero_preventing_spanish_reading_failure2.pdf

American University. (2001). *Teach me different! with Sally L. Smith.* PBS Video (VHS-2pk), Item No. LDES900, Tape 1-LDES 101, Tape 2-LDES 102.

Association for Supervision and Curriculum Development. (February, 2006). *Educational Leadership* (themed issue) "Helping Struggling Students" (various articles/authors).

Chamot, A. U., Huizenga, J., & Hartmann, P.(2005). *Student book, level A, Shining Star.* White Plains, NY: Pearson Education-ESL/Longman.

Chamot, A.U., Keatley, C. W., & Anstrom, K. (2005). *Keys to learning: Skills and strategies for newcomers.* White Plains, NY: Pearson Education-ESL/Longman.

Cline, F. W., & Fay, J. (1990). *Ser padres con amor y lógica: Cómo enseñar responsabilidad a los niños.* Golden, CO: The Love and Logic Press, Inc.

ETA Cuisenaire. (2005). *WorldScapes/Vistas del mundo* (several series of titles). Vernon Hills, IL: Author.

Fay, J., & Funk, D. (1995). *Teaching with love and logic.* Golden, CO: The Love and Logic Press, Inc.

Funk, D. (2002). *Love and logic solutions for kids with special needs.* Golden, CO: The Love and Logic Press, Inc.

Intel Corporation. (2005). *Intel teach to the future^{TM} professional development program.* Retrieved March 16, 2006 from http://www.intel.com/education.

Kirk, M. (2004) *MisUnderstood minds.* WGBH Boston Video (DVD) UPC 783421350991.

LaVoie, R. (2005a). *Beyond F.A.T. city.* PBS (DVD) UPC 841887005111.

LaVoie, R. (2005b). *Learning disabilities and social skills—Last one picked, first one picked on.* PBS (DVD) UPC 841887005487.

Nasseh, B. (1996). Internet-generation & adult learners will create major challenges for higher education institutions in the 21st century. *Computer-Based Distance Education in Higher Education Institutions in Indiana, a Research Report: Papers in Distance Education.* Retrieved March 16, 2006 from http://www.bsu.edu/classes/nasseh/study/learners.html.

Pearson Education. (2006) *Longman science.* White Plains, NY: Pearson Education-ESL/Longman.

Tomlinson, C. A., & McTighe, J. (2006). *Integrating differentiated instruction and understanding by design.* Alexandria, VA: Association for Supervision and Curriculum Development.

Trehearne, M.P., Healy, L.H., McBain, G., MacGregor, M., & Pynoo, S.G. (2005) *Comprehensive literacy resource for grades 1-2 teachers.* Vernon Hills, IL: ETA Cuisenaire/ Thomson Nelson.

Wiggins, G., & McTighe, J. (2005). *Understanding by design.* (*Expanded* 2nd Edition). Upper Saddle River, NJ: Pearson Education, Inc.

Grandparents Raising Grandchildren: What Educators Should Know

Jane Pemberton
Texas Woman's University
Joyce Rademacher
University of North Texas
Gina Anderson
Texas Woman's University

The number of grandparents raising grandchildren has increased dramatically in the last ten years. According to the 2000 Census, 5.8 million (or 3.6 percent of the 158.9 million people aged 30 and over living in households in the United States) were co-resident grandparents (U.S. Bureau of the Census, 2000). Co-resident grandparents are defined as living with grandchildren younger than 18. Among the co-resident grandparents, 2.4 million individuals were identified as grandparent caregivers, or people who had primary responsibility for their co resident grandchildren younger than 18. Among caregivers who are grandparents, 39 percent had cared for their grandchildren for five or more years.

Also continuing to increase in schools is the number of students who are culturally and linguistically diverse, while teachers overwhelmingly remain monolingual, European-Americans (Cushner, McClelland, & Stafford, 2006; Hodgkinson, 2002; August & Hakuta, 1997). English Language Learners (ELL) have increased by 104% between 1990 to 1999, making them the fastest growing group of students in the United States (National Clearinghouse for Bilingual Education, 1999). According to a report from the National Center for Educational Statistics (1997), only 30% of all teachers have received any professional development in teaching ELL students. A mismatch of cultural and academic expectations can exist when non-English-speaking grandparents are the primary caregivers, and teachers remain monolingual. Grandparents who do not speak English may have a different idea about the role of teachers and their grandchildren, what schools should and should not do, and communication expectations.

Teachers in schools today need to know who they are teaching, what to teach, and how to teach (Kea & Utley, 1998). Students who are ethnically and linguistically diverse need teachers who teach using pedagogy responsive to their unique backgrounds. Non-English speaking grandparents raising their grandchildren need teachers that show respect for the unique needs of their grandchildren, as well as the unique needs of the grandparents in the role of caregivers. In other words, teachers need to adapt curriculum, methodology, materials, and communication strategies to address the students' and grandparents' cultural norms. As students and their families become more diverse, a teacher's role in creating a positive learning environment becomes more challenging. Yet, the joy of learning about a different culture from a non-English speaking grandparent raising a grandchild can also be a direct benefit to a classroom community of learners.

The increase in life expectancy and information that grandparents are living healthier, more active lives may contribute to an increase in the in the number of grandparents raising grandchildren. More grandparents than in earlier years are available and willing to assume child-rearing roles for longer periods of time. This is due, in part, to parents being unavailable or unable to be the primary caretakers. Although this trend is more likely among African American and Latino families, all ethnic groups and all social and economic levels are experiencing a raise in numbers of grandparents caring for grandchildren (Burnette, 1999; Haglund, 2000; Mader, 2001). Caring for grandchildren may become as natural an experience as caring for aging parents has been for middle-aged adults. According to Force, Botsfor, Pisano, and Holbert (2000), the grandmother appears to be the most prevalent caretaker, but a range of relatives (e.g., aunts and great grandparents) may fill the kinship caretaker role. Some grandparents are reported to be as young as 35 and others quite elderly.

Census 2000 asked for individuals to choose one or more races. The report is available on the Census 2000 web site at www.census.gov/population/www/cen2000/briefs.html. For respondents who indicated only one racial identity among the major categories (White, Black or African American, American Indian and Alaska Native, Asian, Native Hawaiian, Other Pacific Islander, and Other), the data suggests certain residential or cultural patterns. There is a large proportion of Asian and Hispanics living in multigenerational households. Asian and Hispanic grandparents were less likely to be responsible for their grandchildren and in some cases may have been dependent themselves. Of the 3.6 percent of all people aged 30 and over who lived with their grandchildren, only 2 percent of non-Hispanic

Whites did so. Higher proportions among other racial and ethnic groups were found: 6 percent of people who were Asian, 8 percent of people who were American Indian and Alaska Native, 8 percent of people who were Black, 8 percent of people who were Hispanic, and 10 percent of people who were Pacific Islanders (Census Bureau, 2000).

The reasons grandparents are raising their grandchildren are diverse. Contributing factors include drug abuse, unemployment, incarceration, child neglect and/or abuse, abandonment, mental health problems, poverty, mental health problems, and teenage pregnancy (Mader, 2001). Haglund (2000) conducted an ethnographic study that included six African American grandmothers parenting their grandchildren due to parental cocaine abuse. Haglund concluded that although parenting grandchildren is not easy and is not always desired by the grandparents, it is often the best alternative for the grandchildren, who can then remain in their own families.

Many grandparents find themselves faced with financial burdens, time and energy issues, a lack of acceptance in the new role by family members and friends, and the opportunity to make a difference in their grandchild's life, including at school. Educators need to support grandparents in locating and/or providing appropriate resources and services (Force, Botsfor, Pisano, & Holbert, 2000). According to Beltran (2002), schools should include relative caregivers in the process of developing Individual Education Plans (IEPs) and other activities that typically include parents. Support groups for grandparents are a useful forum for caregivers to share problems, joys, and information about resources (Gabel & Kotsch, 1981; Meyer & Vadasy, 1986; Beltran, 2002).

This study examined various factors that grandparents identify as important to a successful school/home partnership. The purpose of this study was two-fold: First, to gather grandparents' perceptions on the positive aspects and concerns regarding raising their grandchildren. Second, to identify school roadblocks and ways the school can assist them in successfully educating their grandchildren.

Method

Participants

Twenty grandparents were recruited to participate in focus groups. Focus groups are carefully planned discussions that take place in a nonthreatening environment for the purpose of obtaining participants' perceptions on a defined area of interest (Krueger, 1988). The 20 grandparents were recruited from four schools (two elementary and two middle schools) in which principals expressed significant interest in the project. One of the elementary schools was located in a large urban school district and one was located in a suburban district. The two middle schools were located in two separate rural districts. All schools were located in the southwestern region of the United States.

The principal at each school served as the contact persons for recruiting grandparents in their respective buildings. Thus, grandparents were selected from a voluntary pool of grandparents who met the researchers' criteria for being the primary caretaker for his/her grandchild.

The participants' ages ranged from 46 to 78 (M = 62). Twelve participants were European American, four were African American, two were Latino American, and two were American Indian. The group was comprised of five men and 15 women. Grandparents were assigned focus group membership according to the geographical location of their grandchild's school. Focus groups ranged in size from three to nine.

Setting

Focus group meetings with grandparents were held during school hours in a vacant room in each of the participating schools. The grandparents and the researchers sat around a table.

Focus Group Questions

Four questions were prepared prior to the focus group meetings. Questions 1 and 2 related to the personal aspects of raising their grandchild. Questions 3 and 4 related to school issues associated with educating their grandchild. Specifically, Question 1 asked grandparents what they believed to be the positive aspects of raising a grandchild. After each question was posed, grandparents wrote their responses onto note cards. They were instructed to write one idea per card. After responses to Question 1 and Question 2 were collected and discussed, Question 3 and Question 4 were posed. Specifically, Question 3 asked grandparents to identify what school roadblocks they encountered while Question 4 asked them to list what the school could do to assist them. Once again, grandparents were asked to write one idea per card.

Measurement and Procedures

Measures. Two systems were used to record responses during the group meetings. Participants wrote statements representing their responses to a particular question on a 3" by 5" note card. Other verbal responses were transcribed by a note-taker.

During each focus group meeting, questions were posed one at a time by a researcher who served as moderator. After each question had been posed, participants wrote their responses onto note cards. Each grandparent could write as many responses (i.e., complete as many cards) as he or she chose. The note cards were collected by the moderator, and the response to each statement on the card was discussed by the group.

As they discussed the cards, the focus group members organized them into categories by topic. After all the cards had been discussed and categorized, each category was given a label by the group. For example, the responses, "Call me at once, I have a mobile and phone at home," "Make every effort to get fathers involved," and "Be willing to communicate" might receive the category label "Encourage Communication." The group moderator wrote a category label on a card and posted it next to the appropriate cluster of responses. Each member then voted on how important they believed each category to be with "1" being unimportant to "7" being very important. A note-taker transcribed the responses related to each category.

Procedures. Four focus groups of three to nine grandparents were formed from the pool of 20 volunteers. Each meeting lasted two hours. Three researchers were present, two sharing the role of moderator, and the other as note taker.

The standard protocol for the four meetings was the same. The first fifteen minutes consisted of a welcome by the moderator, the introduction of group members, an overview of the purpose of the study, and an explanation of the research procedures that included the ground rules for discussion. If an individual needed help to write ideas onto cards, one of the researchers sitting near the person would serve as a scribe.

The ground rules for discussion were based on the Metaplan procedures for focus group meetings (Schnelle & Stoltz, 1987; Vance, 1995). Using the Metaplan steps, a question is stated, participants write their thoughts and feelings onto cards with one idea per card and using seven words or less when possible. After the showing of responses, the moderator collects the card and displays them on the wall. The moderator, with the participants' help, organizes the note cards into clusters or categories with participants continuing to write more thoughts during this process. After a discussion of thoughts, feelings, and ideas regarding each category, participants vote on the category that best reflects how they feel. Figure 1 depicts an example of how to use the Metaplan steps.

Figure 1. Metaplan steps as a process to record responses during the group meetings.

METAPLAN STEPS

Step 1   The question is stated.

Step 2   Participants write thoughts and feelings on note cards.

Step 3	Participants write clearly and neatly. Misspellings are okay.
Step 4	Write one idea per card.
Step 5	Use 7 words or less, if possible.
Step 6	Moderator collects and reads note cards aloud and displays them on the wall.
Step 7	Moderator, with participants help, organizes the note cards into clusters or categories of thought, feelings, and opinions.
Step 8	Participants may continue writing their thoughts during this process.
Step 9	The moderator and participants discuss their thoughts, feelings, and ideas.
Step 10	The participants conclude the process by rating the categories according to how they feel about the importance of each category.

Results

The researchers examined the categories of focus group responses by each geographical group of grandparents. The written responses were coded for each research question. For Question 1 (What are the positive aspects of raising a grandchild?), eight categories of responses emerged as shown in Table 1 (see Table 1). The responses indicated that grandparents value the opportunity to give guidance and provide stability. They also feel a sense of pride and satisfaction relating to making a difference in their grandchild's life. In addition, grandparents indicated the positive nature of having a second chance at parenting while watching their grandchildren grow into productive citizens.

Table 1
Mean Ratings on Categories of Responses by Grandparents on the Positive Aspects of Raising a Grandchild (N = 20)

Category	N	M	Sample Comments
Giving Guidance	6	7.0	"I teach him to do what is right."
Providing Stability	5	7.0	"Knowing that they are safe."
Feeling Pride/Satisfaction	5	7.0	"Know we made a difference in their
Giving Love	17	6.8	lives."
Learning From Them	14	6.5	"To let them know love and they are
Watching Them Grow	18	6.5	not thrown away."
Having a Second/Third			"I've become a softer person, more
Chance	11	6.3	understanding."
Receiving Love	9	5.4	"Seeing them grown into productive
			citizens."
			"I love being a mom again!"
			"The unconditional love he gives me"

N = number of responses written by grandparents
M = mean rating of importance (1 is low importance and 7 is high importance)

Table 2
Mean Ratings on Categories of Responses by Grandparents on Concerns of Raising a Grandchild (N = 20)

Category	N	M	Sample Comments
Dealing with Future			"Proper way to direct them in life"
Concerns	7	6.9	"Living long enough to finish the job"
Dealing with Life Span			"Trying to keep up with their young
Issues	13	6.8	activities"
Supporting education			"Teaching them how to handle hurt"
issues	4	6.8	"No time for self"

Dealing with emotional issues	25	6.8	"Legal ramifications if not adopted or full guardianship"
Time	17	6.2	"Having adequate financial resources"
Feeling a lack of control	23	6.2	
Resolving financial issues	3	6.1	

N = number of responses written by grandparents
M = mean rating of importance (1 is low importance and 7 is high importance)

For Question 2 (What concerns do you have raising a grandchild?), seven categories of responses emerged as shown in Table 2 (see Table 2 above). The responses indicated that grandparents were concerned about the future, including lifespan issues as in living long enough to raise their grandchild. They also expressed that it was sometimes difficult to keep up with activities designed for younger children and adults. One grandmother reported her grandchild typically wanted to go to McDonalds after a school game with the other students, but that the grandmother wanted to go home and not join the other families. Grandparents reported they needed support dealing with emotional issues for their grandchildren, and were concerned with teasing. In addition, grandparents responded that time was a concern, as in having time for self or for friends that did not have grandchildren in their homes. Legal and financial issues were also discussed, as the plans that were made during retirement years had changed. Grandparents expressed concerns of signing for a grandchild at school, having medical support, and guardianship for protection of the grandchild.

Table 3 *Mean Ratings on Categories of Responses by Grandparents on School Roadblocks Grandparents Encounter (N = 20)*

Category	N	M	Sample Comments
Knowing Grandchild's			"Knowing peers' family"
Friends and Family	8	7.0	"Not being able to sign for the
School System	7	7.0	grandchildren"
Schoolwork Concerns	12	6.9	"Staying knowledgeable about subject
Increasing Communication	10	6.8	areas"
Building Respectful			"Lack of understanding from teachers"
Partnerships	27	6.5	"Keeping family matters private"

N = number of responses written by grandparents
M = mean rating of importance (1 is low importance and 7 is high importance)

For Question 3 (What school roadblocks do grandparents encounter?), seven categories of responses emerged as shown in Table 3 (see Table 3 above). The responses indicated that grandparents were concerned about knowing their grandchild's friends and the friends' families. Grandparents wanted teachers to have understanding about the grandchild's situation, but to keep the information private. Building respectful partnerships was a key area. Grandparents related incidents where they did not feel valued as a caregiver, and expressed a frustration at the perceived lack of respect that was given by teachers. For example, one grandparent reported, "The school doesn't know what to do with us." Another grandparent reported, "The teacher disliked my granddaughter because of her mother." Grandparents also expressed that it was difficult to support the grandchildren with homework. One grandparent suggested, "The teacher should make sure he knows how to do the homework."

Table 4
Mean Ratings on Categories of Responses by Grandparents on How the School Can Assist Grandparents (N = 20)

Category	N	M	Sample Comments
Providing Tutoring	7	7.0	"Provide after school help, homework,
Using Quality Instruction	10	6.9	etc."
Offering Counseling			"Work on comprehension issues"
Support	3	6.9	"Provide counseling support for
Increasing Teacher			grandchild"
Awareness	16	6.9	"Teachers need to know the
Encouraging			background of children"
Communication	22	6.7	"Confidentiality – Keep our business
Supporting the Grandchild	7	6.4	private but be willing to communicate"
Offering Support Groups	4	6.4	"Be sensitive to grandchild's situation."
			"Support groups/reaffirming parenting skills"

N = number of responses written by grandparents
M = mean rating of importance (1 is low importance and 7 is high importance)

For Question 4 (How can the school assist you?), seven categories of responses emerged as shown in Table 4 (see Table 4 above). The responses indicated that grandparents want quality instruction. They were interested in support through tutoring opportunities. Counseling of the grandchild in the school, learning about the unique needs (including special education needs), and attending support groups for grandparents raising their grandchild were all suggested by grandparents. The category of ongoing communication was important. Again, grandparents expressed the need to "Keep our business private." One grandparent reported there was often a story as to why the grandparents were raising their grandchild, and that should not be discussed in the teacher's lounge.

Discussion

Many of the grandparents interviewed were raising a second family without any extended family or community supports. Schools can create additional, often unintended obstacles for grandparents. Helping with homework can be daunting and difficult for grandparents and the students. One grandparent reported, "But grandpa, that isn't the way we do it in school." The grandfather answered, "Well, 2 plus 2 is always 4." Another grandparent wrote: "Homework. I went to school 50 years ago. I forgot all that." One grandparent requested "more information on the assignment sheet." Another grandparent reported, "Homework can take from right after school to 9:00 p.m. to get it done. It is important that teachers send homework home that is at the independent level of instruction for the student, with clear directions and a keen awareness of the time it will take to complete the homework assignment."

Sending notes home addressed to parents, for some reflected a lack of respect of the role of the grandparent. "When they make family assignments, remember we are grands." "When sending notes home, it is for Mom/Dad activities." The responses highlight the importance of increasing respectful communication between the school and the home.

Grandparents also referred to respect with communication: "Respect me as a parent." "Listen to my input. I know this child." "Admit that we know a little about what the kids are about."

"Learn to listen." The grandparents' responses indicated a need for educators to review communication between home and school and monitor communication so ensure it is positive with grandparents, as well as all caregivers of students in the classroom. "We want her to know our culture" was the response of one grandparent. She reported it was natural in their community, and the grandchild can listen to the stories of the family and learn. This grandparent described the grandchild as having the chance to garden with the grandparents, with the grandfather digging the hole for the plant and the granddaughter covering it up. This grandparent reported raising a grandchild was "My way to help get through it (problems with her parents)."

Grandparents that participated in the focus groups appeared to appreciate the opportunity to provide information to the researchers on ways schools could support grandparents raising their grandchildren. It is important in any school community to identify the grandparents raising their grandchildren, and to offer supports such as tutoring, support groups, and respectful communication. An activity as the Metaplan could be used by educators to identify the unique needs of grandparents in their school community.

Summary and implications for practice

As this research indicates, listening to grandparents' voices is an important source of information to guide educators interested in reform issues associated with the call for more parent/family involvement in today's schools. For example, the grandparents stated that they had knowledge about their grandchild and desired to be seen and heard as a valuable member in the educational process. Teacher educators should be aware that grandparents have unique skills and needs and fill an important role as caregiver and supporter for the students. Teachers should continue to investigate communication strategies aimed at building better partnerships.

Some grandparents were frustrated with a lack of understanding from teachers and expressed a desire to build respectful partnerships. Confidentiality was a high concern, with one grandparent reporting that she did not want the reason she was raising her grandchild discussed in the teacher's lounge. Teachers need to be sensitive to the histories of families and express a willingness to maintain confidentiality of family matters and treat everyone with respect.

Grandparents also reported when teachers provided quality instruction, ongoing communication, and tutoring opportunities, their grandchildren benefited. In addition, grandparents expressed interest in teachers being aware that their grandchild was being raised by grandparents. Teachers should consider support groups for grandparents that provide opportunities to share their expertise, identify resources, and provide fellowship.

Suggestions for educators who have non-English-speaking grandparents raising their grandchildren include the following:

- Establish methods of communication that support non-English-speaking grandparents and their grandchildren.
- Identify interpreters from the educational community and community-at-large, and have an interpreter available for informal as well as formal meetings. Written

communication should be in the primary language of the grandparent, as well as in English.

- If possible, make a home visit. Make arrangements prior to the home visit with the grandparents, grandchildren, and interpreter.

- Be aware of spoken and written language needs and respond to unique communication requirements. In one community, most families had a VCR, but no telephone. Teachers had videotapes available for check out by the students, so families could observe activities in the classroom and the child could describe activities and learning experiences in the classroom and school to their non-English-speaking grandparents.

- Identify non-English-speaking grandparents' perceptions of school and communicate clearly expectations and available supports.

- Communicate the importance of involvement by families in American education.

- Be welcoming in actions and environment. From the entry to the school, to help in finding the location of the grandchild's classroom, to a comfortable chair for adults in the classroom, teachers should create an inviting classroom and school environment.

- Communicate expectations of the school by addressing an issue directly and offering support. One non-English-speaking grandparent was hesitant to get her grandchild up in the morning, insisting that sleep was important. After the teacher explained the importance of beginning the school day with the rest of the students, and providing the grandchild with a strategy to wake up (alarm clock) in the morning, the tardy issue was resolved.

- Make it as convenient as possible for non-English-speaking grandparents to participate in meetings and activities.
- Arrange transportation. Often non-English-speaking grandparents do not communicate that they need transportation. Arrange for transportation prior to scheduled time. One grandparent lived within walking distance of the school, but was caring for an infant in the home and needed a stroller to be able to go to the school.
- Be aware of child care issues with the family. Some grandparents are raising grandchildren with a wide age range, and may be also caring for other members of the family.
- Schedule meetings at convenient times for grandparents.
- Make sure meetings meet the needs of the student and grandparent by providing an agenda and information about who will be attending, and explaining what non-English-speaking grandparents can expect during the meeting.
- Refrain from making generalizations about members of ethnic, cultural, or linguistic groups that may not address each individual in the group.
- Identify your own stereotypes and recognize that your assumptions could change your own behavior. For example, a teacher might not invite a non-English-speaking grandparent to go on a field trip or to bring snacks, not wanting to add to the responsibilities of the grandparent. In fact, the grandparent may want to be involved in the

classroom and the invitation to join the group would be welcome.

- Remember that families are not homogeneous, and grandparents raising grandchildren are not a homogenous group either.
- Know that courts often appoint grandparents as legal guardians of their grandchildren, and support grandparents' willingness to provide care.
- Value the contributions and experiences non-English-speaking grandparents offer their grandchildren and the educational community. One school administrator reported she had to work at thinking of grandparents raising grandchildren as more than temporary volunteers.
- Offer resources to grandparents ranging from workshops on legal issues to signing for their grandchildren in school.
- Work in a positive, encouraging manner with grandchildren and their non-English-speaking grandparents.
- Demonstrate respect at all levels. If appropriate, ask the grandchild for suggestions to support the non-English-speaking grandparents. Often the grandchild has an insight into ways educators can positively include their family members in meetings and activities.
- Recognize the unique strengths of the non-English-speaking grandparents offer, and celebrate the diversity in today's schools by working together with all members of the school community.

A number of resources are available on the web. AARP Grandparent Information Center (GIC), which provides information about services and programs to help improve the lives of grandparent-headed households at gic@aarp.org; Generations United, which focuses solely on promoting intergenerational strategies, programs, and policies at www.gu.org; Grandparent Again, which offers information about education, legal support, support groups, and other organizations for grandparents raising grandchildren at www.grandparentagain.com; and GrandsPlace, which offers support to grandparents and other relatives raising others' children at www.grandplace.org.

References

August, D., & Hakuta, K. (1997). *Improving schooling for language-minority children: A research agenda.* Washington, DC: National Academy Press.

Bauer, A.M., & Shea, T.M. (2003). *Parents and schools: Creating a successful partnership for students with special needs.* Columbus, OH: Merrill Prentice Hall.

Beltran, A. (2002). *Grandparents and other relatives raising children: Access to education.* Generations United. Retrieved March 17, 2006 from www.gu.org.

Burnette, D. (1999). Custodial grandparents in Latino families: Patterns of service use and predicators of unmet service needs. *Social Work, 44,* 22-34.

Cushner, K., McClelland, A., & Safford, P. (2006). *Human diversity in education: An integrative approach.* Boston: McGraw-Hill.

Force, L.T., Botsford, A., Pisano, P.A., & Holbert, A. (2000). Grandparents raising children with and without a developmental disability: Preliminary comparisons. *Journal of Gerontological Social Work, 33*(4), 5-21.

Gabel, H., & Kotsch, L.S. (1981). Extended families and young handicapped children. *Topics in Early Childhood Special Education, 1,* 29-35.

Generations United Fact Sheet: Grandparents and other relatives raising children: Challenges of caring for the second family. Retrieved March 17, 2006 from www.gu.org.

Haglund, K. (2000). Parenting a second time around: An ethnography of African American grandmothers parenting grandchildren due to parental cocaine abuse. *Journal of Family Nursing, 6*(2), 120-126.

Hodgkinson, H. (2002). Demographics and teacher education: An overview. *Journal of Teacher Education, 53,* 102-105.

Kea, C.D., & Utley, C.A. (1998). To teach me is to know me. *Journal of Special Education, 32*(1), 44-47.

National Center for Educational Statistics. (1997). *1993-94 Schools and staffing survey: A profile of policies and practices for limited English proficient students: Screening methods program support, and teacher training.* Washington, DC: U.S. Department of Education, Office of Educational Research and Improvement.

National Clearinghouse for Bilingual Education (1999). *The growing numbers of limited English proficient.* Washington, DC: U.S. Department of Education.

Mader, S.L. (2001). Grandparents raising grandchildren. *The Delta Kappa Gamma Bulletin*, Fall, p. 33-35.

Meyer, D., & Vadasy, P. (1986). *Grandparents workshops: How to organize workshops for grandparents of children with handicaps.* Seattle: University of Washington Press.

Schnelle, W., & Stoltz, I. (1987). *The metaplan method: Communication tools for planning learning groups* (Metaplan Series No. 7). Goethestrasse, Germany.

U.S. Bureau of the Census.(2000). *Statistical abstracts of the United States.* Washington, DC: U.S. Government Printing Office.

Vance, M. (1995). *Getting to know you: Knowing myself and my students to guide learning* (Strategram 7[2]). Lawrence: University of Kansas Center for Research on Learning.

Call for Manuscripts

The real world of school in the United States is one of much cultural, linguistic, and academic diversity where students of numerous cultural and language groups believe that the educators who teach them will possess adequate knowledge about their experiences, beliefs, values and educational needs to facilitate educational success. While the teaching force in the United States continues to reflect little diversity, it has been estimated that 70% of teachers who work with the linguistically diverse student population have had no training in bilingual or ESL education. It is significant that newcomers as well as culturally diverse students who were born in the United States and teachers may have quite different notions regarding what should occur at school and in the classroom. In order to compensate for the mismatch of a diverse student population and a teacher corps that lacks diversity, it is imperative that appropriate and effective teacher preparation be provided.

The knowledgeable and caring educator of diverse populations embarks on a journey of discovery about self and others, developing a sense of intercultural understanding that guides perception and critical educational decisions. Intercultural understanding implies an understanding of language and how it is used in relationships. It includes an understanding of the dynamic nature of culture in general and the knowledge that there is difference and variety within and among various cultural groups. Intercultural understanding entails a willingness to be a student of diverse cultures and their component languages, behaviors, values, and beliefs. When students perceive that a teacher has chosen to learn about his or her unique life experiences, they sense that they are welcome in the classroom. Similarly, students who see themselves reflected in the school curriculum tend to believe that school is a place for them. The expectation is that as intercultural understanding increases, academic achievement is enhanced.

Therefore, the Bilingual/ESL Committee of the Federation of North Texas Area Universities proposes to prepare a monograph entitled *Intercultural Understanding*. Second in a series of monographs addressing critical issues in the education of English language learners, the monograph will be a compendium of information, current trends, and research associated with exploring and promoting intercultural understanding. In addition a discussion of the impact of intercultural sensitivity and understanding on best practices in bilingual and ESL education will be included. The anticipated audience for the monograph will be preservice and inservice teachers and administrators in addition to university faculty and students.

Interested authors are invited to submit scholarly papers on topics related to intercultural understanding as well as best practice in the bilingual and/or ESL classroom. Suggested topics include culturally relevant and culturally responsive teaching, administering diverse populations, error analysis and comparative analysis of English and other languages, multicultural education and the English language learner, cross-cultural communication, dichos and proverbs, ESL and content area instruction, language policy in the United States, bilingual and ESL programs that have incorporated intercultural understanding into the curriculum, book reviews, and ESL and the newcomer. For more information you may contact Dr. Melinda Cowart, Managing Editor, at mcowart@mail.twu.edu or Dr. Phap Dam, Series Editor, at pdam@mail.twu.edu. The deadline for submission is November 15, 2006. Guidelines for authors follow.

256

Guidelines for Authors

Manuscripts must adhere to the following guidelines:

1. Length: The manuscript, including references, charts and tables should not exceed 20 typewritten pages.
2. Type: The document should be completed in Microsoft Word. The font should be 12 point and in Times New Roman.
3. Style: Manuscripts must conform to the Publication Manual of the American Psychological Association (APA), 5th edition (2001).
4. Cover letter: Include a cover letter explaining the relationship of your scholarly paper to the theme of the monograph. Provide a statement indicating that the paper is original material and is not under consideration for publication elsewhere.
5. Title Page: Include the following information on a separate page:
   Title of manuscript
   Author's name
   Complete mailing address
   E-mail address
   Business and home phone numbers
   Institutional affiliation and address
   Biographical data about each author
6. Abstract: Submit an abstract of 100-150 words.
7. Miscellaneous: Spelling, grammar, and accuracy of references are the responsibility of the authors.
8. Copies: Submit two double-spaced paper copies of the manuscript along with an e-mail attachment to Dr. Melinda Cowart, Managing Editor, (mcowart@mail.twu.edu). Copies submitted for consideration for publication will not be returned. Deadline: November 15, 2006
9. Book Reviews: Book reviews should be in APA format and no longer than 5 pages in length.

Authors' Information

Dr. Phap Dam, a native of Vietnam, is professor and coordinator of the Bilingual and ESL Education Program in the Department of Teacher Education at Texas Woman's University. His areas of expertise include second-language acquisition theories and practices, multicultural education, and comparative linguistics. He has published monographs and articles in language education, translated Spanish poetry into Vietnamese, and spoken at state, national, and international conferences on language education. Dr. Dam is the series editor for the current series of monographs on issues affecting English language learners and their teachers.

Dr. Melinda T. Cowart began her career in bilingual education in 1975. She has been a bilingual educator in elementary school, an ESL teacher in middle school and is currently an associate professor of teacher education in the bilingual program at Texas Woman's University. She and her husband, Mr. Ron Cowart, have worked extensively with refugee youth and adults. Her research interests include the effective, equitable education for linguistically and ethnically diverse students and the appropriate preparation of teachers who will be teaching diverse populations. Dr. Cowart is managing editor for the current series of monographs on issues affecting English language learners and their teachers.

Dr. Wayne E. Wright is an assistant professor of Bicultural-Bilingual Studies at the University of Texas, San Antonio. He is the co-director of the Language Policy Research Unit of the Educational Policy Studies Laboratory at Arizona State University, serves as the co-chair of the Language Policy special interest group of the National Association for Bilingual Education, and serves as an Executive Board Member and Vice President for Publications for the National Association for the Education and Advancement of Cambodian, Laotian, and Vietnamese Americans.

Dr. Patsy J. Robles-Goodwin is an assistant professor in Early Childhood Education at the University of North Texas. She is a former elementary bilingual/ESL teacher and school administrator. Her research interests include educational issues affecting Latino families and students, young children and linguistic/literacy issues, and diversity teaching and training.

Dr. Deyoe-Chiullan is married and the mother of two young adult sons who have been educated in Texas public schools. She has taught in bilingual schools and teacher education programs in Kansas, Illinois, Texas, and Colombia (South America) for the past 37 years. She is fluent and literate in Spanish and English. Since retirement from the Texas public school system, she teaches as an adjunct professor at Southern Methodist University and Richland College and provides expert tutoring to candidates seeking test-based teacher certification in Texas.

Dr. Luis A. Rosado directs the Center for Bilingual Education Program at the University of Texas at Arlington. He holds degrees from the University of Puerto Rico, Boston State College and Texas A & M University-Kingsville. He has published in the areas of parental involvement, cross-cultural communication, and Spanish linguistics. Dr. Rosado has 22 years of teaching experience at the elementary, high school and college levels. He has taught in Puerto Rico, Massachusetts, and Texas.

Dr. Eva Midobuche has been in the field of bilingual education since 1976. She is currently an associate professor of Bilingual Education and Diversity Studies at Texas Tech University College of Education. Her research interests include the preparation of teachers to educate culturally and linguistically diverse students, multicultural education, and teaching the content areas to English language learners. Dr. Midobuche has held teaching and/or administrative appointments at Arizona State University, University of Oklahoma, and University of Texas at El Paso.

260

Dr. Alfredo H. Benavides is professor and academic program coordinator of the Bilingual Education and Diversity Studies Program in the College of Education at Texas Tech University. He is also the co-editor of the *Bilingual Research Journal*. Dr. Benavides has been in the field of bilingual education for over 30 years and his publications are numerous. His research interests include the preparation of bilingual and ESL education teachers, multicultural education, and bilingual education policy.

Dr. Gina Anderson is an assistant professor in the Department of Teacher Education at Texas Woman's University. Her areas of expertise and scholarship include curriculum and instruction, middle level education, educational foundations, and multicultural/diversity issues.

Dr. Janelle Mathis, an associate professor, teaches graduate and undergraduate courses in literacy instruction for diverse classrooms and children's literature at the University of North Texas. Her research interests include the selection and use of children's literature about issues of identity, diversity, social justice, and the global society.

Dr. Mary F. B. Garza is an assistant professor at Texas Woman's University. A classroom teacher for 13 years, Dr. Garza has also worked in the Texas Education Agency with both the Division of Migrant Education and the Bilingual Education Program. Her research interests include the use of music and writing with language development in the bilingual classroom, distance learning with migrant and bilingual early education, parental involvement, and teacher preparation.

Dr. Jane B. Pemberton is an associate professor in the Special Education Program, Department of Teacher Education, College of Professional Education, Texas Woman's University. Her research interests include instructional strategies for all learners, inclusive practices, and curriculum-based assessment.

Dr. Chris Green is an assistant professor at Texas A & M University-Commerce and serves as director of the bilingual/ESL teacher preparation program. A former bilingual elementary and high school ESL teacher, elementary principal, and bilingual and special education coordinator, she also served twelve years as an education associate for the Intercultural Development Research Association (IDRA). Her research interests include biliteracy development (English and Spanish) and technology tools for first and second language and literacy development.

Dr. Claudia Sanchez is assistant professor and project director of Bilingual/ESL grants at Texas Woman's University. Her areas of interest are Spanish/English literacy development, Bilingual/ESL teaching methodologies, and crosscultural issues in education.

Dr. Joyce Ann Rademacher is an associate professor of special education at the University of North Texas. She prepares teachers to teach students with mild/moderate disabilities. Her research interests include the development and validation of strategic interventions for diverse learners in inclusive settings.